THE LIGHTNING-FAST FIELD GUIDE TO THE BIBLE

THE LIGHTNING-FAST FIELD GUIDE TO THE BIBLE

YOUR COMPACT COMPANION FOR EXPLORING THE BEST BOOK EVER

MATT WHITMAN

ZONDERVAN BOOKS

ZONDERVAN BOOKS

The Lightning-Fast Field Guide to the Bible

Published by Zondervan, 3950 Sparks Drive SE, Suite 101, Grand Rapids, MI 49546, USA. Zondervan is a registered trademark of The Zondervan Corporation, L.L.C., a wholly owned subsidiary of HarperCollins Christian Publishing, Inc.

Requests for information should be addressed to customercare@harpercollins.com.

Zondervan titles may be purchased in bulk for educational, business, fundraising, or sales promotional use. For information, please email SpecialMarkets@Zondervan.com.

ISBN 978-0-310-36978-3 (audio)

Library of Congress Cataloging-in-Publication Data

Names: Whitman, Matt, 1975- author
Title: The lightning-fast field guide to the Bible : your compact companion for exploring the best book ever / Matt Whitman.
Description: Grand Rapids MI : Zondervan Books, [2026]
Identifiers: LCCN 2025042204 (print) | LCCN 2025042205 (ebook) | ISBN 9780310369769 trade paperback | ISBN 9780310369776 ebook
Subjects: LCSH: Bible—Introductions
Classification: LCC BS475.3 .W528 2026 (print) | LCC BS475.3 (ebook) | DDC 220.6/1—dc23/eng/20251114
LC record available at https://lccn.loc.gov/2025042204
LC ebook record available at https://lccn.loc.gov/2025042205

Author represented by The Steve Laube Agency.

HarperCollins Publishers, Macken House, 39/40 Mayor Street Upper, Dublin 1, D01 C9W8, Ireland (https://www.harpercollins.com)

Cover design: Bethany Gano
Interior illustrations: The Ten Minute Bible Hour Team
Interior design: Kait Lamphere

CONTENTS

PREFACE

No matter where you are in your journey with God and the Bible, this book is written with you in mind.

You may be someone who's brand-new to the Bible and feels a little overwhelmed at the prospect of exploring this huge, ancient book.

This book is going to help you with that.

You might be someone who's getting into the Bible often, but you're a little embarrassed that you zone out sometimes and don't always track with what you're seeing.

This book is going to help you with that.

You might be someone who's read the Bible in little pieces again and again over the course of your life, but now you're wanting to see how it all fits together from the ten-thousand-foot view.

This book is going to help you with that.

You might be someone who studies and teaches from the Bible for a living, but from time to time, you'd like to be able to reach for a super-quick resource to help jog your memory on parts of the Bible you haven't visited for quite a while.

This book is going to help you with that.

You're right to want to venture deeper into the Bible. There's a reason it's the most famous, most purchased, most gifted, most influential book of all time. It credibly holds itself out as being from the one true God, and what's more, you're part of the story.

It's an anthology of books written by very different people under very different circumstances over a very long period of time, but the whole thing hangs together with amazing cohesion. It's just short enough that, with effort, you can make a mental map of it all and hold the whole thing in your mind at once, but it's just long enough that you're going to discover tons of new connections every time you walk through it again.

The Bible is God's sweeping, epic story of creation, calamity, and a crippling curse that eventually gets broken when the hero crushes evil once and for all. It's a lot, and this guide is meant to provide markers along the way to help you stay oriented as you explore.

This book is built to be a nimble, content-rich breakdown of each book of the Bible that uses normal-person language to succinctly cover the big, important, obvious stuff and also take you into the equally important, less obvious stuff. You won't need instructions on how to use the book in your hands; just open it up and you'll know what to do.

Godspeed, explorer!

VITAL STATS

Position: 1 of 66.
Chapters: 50.
Verses: 1,533.
Word Count: 32,046 (2/66).
Most-Used Words: God, father, lord, sons, land.
Group: The books of Moses. Also called The Law, The Pentateuch, The Torah, The First Five Books of the Hebrew Bible.
Audience: Ancient Hebrews (and their kids) who escaped Egypt.
Date: Between 1400 and 1200 BC.
Popularity Rank: 5 of 66.

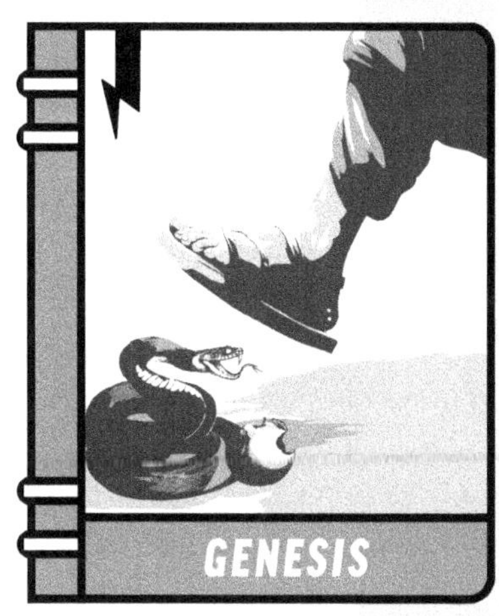

GENESIS

Lightning-Fast Summary: An ancient book describing even more ancient things. God makes everything out of nothing, then the people He formed reject Him and wreck creation. Rather than quitting, God starts a plan to fix it all.

Unique Feature: The sheer amount of time covered is unlike anything else in the Bible. Genesis covers more time than the rest of the Bible combined, and more than all the time that has passed from the end of the book until right now.

Who Wrote It? Moses.

When the Events Happened: From time immemorial to 1800ish BC.

Years Covered: A lot.

Original Language: Hebrew, except for two Aramaic words in chapter 31.

Original Audience: Former Hebrew slaves wandering in the desert, descended from the characters in this book.

Type of Book: History narrative with other stuff mixed in, including poetry, prophecy, blessings, and curses.

Tone and Feel: Sweeping, dramatic, epic; peppered with irony, humor, and close-up, personal moments.

Where It's Set: All over the ancient world, including modern-day Iraq, Jordan, Syria, Turkey, Lebanon, Saudi Arabia, Egypt, and Israel. The story flows from east to west, just like the language in which it is written.

Stuff You Can Still Physically Look At: Genesis is *very* old, so not much is left from that time, but it's possible that the cave of Machpelah in Hebron is the actual place where Abraham is buried.

Parts You Might Recognize Even If You Haven't Read the Bible: Creation, Adam and Eve in the garden of Eden, the Tower of Babel, Noah's ark, Jacob and Esau, and Joseph and the coat of many colors.

Important Characters: God is the most important character in Genesis and the entire Bible. Leading human characters: Adam and Eve, Cain and Abel, Noah, Abraham and Sarah, and their descendants—Isaac, Jacob, and then Joseph and his brothers in Egypt.

Story Arc: Genesis starts at the grandest level imaginable and then narrows all the way in on one guy and his family.

The Very Beginning: Genesis opens before existence, but God is there. He uses His mind and unlimited power to make existence out of nothing. Humans—those whom God makes in His image—are the crowning bit of creation. Adam and Eve are with God in the garden of Eden. God commissions them to enjoy it and cultivate beautiful things. God sizes it up and says the whole thing is good.

The Curse That Sets Up the Tension of the Whole Bible: However, there's a subversive serpent living in the garden. He hates God, and because of that, he hates the people made in God's image. The serpent tricks Adam and Eve into eating from a tree God told them not to eat from. The fruit from that tree gives them the knowledge of good and evil—a tool too sharp for humans to wield. It's the first sin, and with it comes a calamitous ripple effect. That single action puts imperfection, decay, suffering, guilt, shame, and death into the world for everyone, and there's nothing Adam and Eve can do to break the curse.

What God Decides to Do About It: Now, only a few pages into the Bible, is the decisive moment that'll determine the outcome of everything. Will God wad up His damaged creation and start over, or will He keep and fix it?

He chooses the second option.

God condemns the snake, and says the snake will have its heyday, but promises in the end there will be One descended from Eve who will crush the serpent's head and defeat the curse.

God Picks Abraham: Adam and Eve have kids and grandkids, but as humans spread, so does the curse. The heart of humanity is afflicted with the incurable disease of sin. Nothing they try can fix it. God sends a flood as judgment for evil, but the survivors go right back to disobeying God.

Several generations later, we meet a guy named Abraham. For whatever reason, God picks him and promises to make him great, give him a land, and make his descendants into a great nation. God will bless them, and *through* Abraham's descendants, all the nations will be blessed.

Abraham gets a lot of stuff right and a lot of stuff wrong, but the one redeeming thing about him is that *he believes God,* and God credits that to him as righteousness.

The last third of Genesis follows Abraham's kids, grandkids, and great-grandkids all the way to Egypt, where they've been blessed in spite of their mistakes, and where the ancient promise of One who will defeat the curse is reiterated.

The Plot at the End: We've got a horrific hereditary curse plaguing humanity, but we've also got a hopeful hereditary promise of redemption through Abraham's flawed family.

Theme: Even when Abraham and his family are unfaithful, God is faithful. He will redeem the mess and defeat the curse because of His character and in spite of human resistance.

Key Verse: Genesis 1:1—"In the beginning God created the heavens and the earth."

What Would Happen If Genesis Weren't in the Bible? The rest of the Bible wouldn't make sense. Genesis explains where the problem of sin and death (the curse) comes from, how serious it is, and how God will fix it.

Most Shocking Moments: When God creates everything out of nothing. Or the time Judah sleeps with his daughter-in-law because he thinks she's a lady of the night.

Unsung Hero: Tamar's shrewdness preserves Judah's line, which eventually leads to the birth of Jesus through her son Perez.

Most Relatable Moment: God tells Sarah she's going to have a baby despite the fact that she's old and can't have kids, and she laughs.

Most Quoted Moment: The first verse—"In the beginning God created the heavens and the earth."

Most Controversial Part: You could fill a stadium with books speculating about how God made everything and how long it took, but Genesis makes no effort to explain any of this in modern scientific terms. Rather, it sums it up in a story and insists that God made everything.

Most Applicable Moment for Modern Audiences: Genesis 3 explains the suffering, toil, and death that define so much of our existence.

If You Don't Have Time to Read the Whole Thing, at Least Read: Genesis 12:1–3.

When You Visualize Genesis, Picture: The serpent (who represents the curse) being crushed by the One whom God promised.

Tomb of the Patriarchs (Cave of Machpelah) is located in the heart of the old city of Hebron. The cave and adjoining field were purchased by Abraham as a burial plot.

Roman Yanushevsky/stock.adobe.com

VITAL STATS

Position: 2 of 66.

Chapters: 40.

Verses: 1213.

Word Count: 25,957 (5/66).

Most-Used Words: Lord, people, gold, Pharaoh, Egypt, tent, made.

Group: The books of Moses. Also called The Law, The Pentateuch, The Torah, The First Five Books of the Hebrew Bible.

Audience: Ancient Hebrews (and their kids) who escaped Egypt.

Date: Between 1400 and 1200 BC.

Popularity Rank: 14 of 66.

EXODUS

Lightning-Fast Summary: God's chosen people are slaves in Egypt, but God raises up Moses to free them by God's miraculous power. After they escape, the Hebrews wander in the wilderness, trying to figure out what it means to be God's chosen people and live by His law.

Unique Feature: The famous event the book is named for only takes up the first third of the book. The remaining two-thirds are the aftermath, as the Hebrews try to figure out what it means to be God's people.

Who Wrote It? Moses, Miriam (his sister who wrote a song in chapter 15), and God (who authored the Ten Commandments).

Original Language: Hebrew.

When the Events Happened: Some smart people who do this for a living think the 1500s and 1400s BC. Others think the 1200s BC.

Years Covered: At least 400, but with a focus on about 85 years.

Historical Setting: The New Kingdom era of Egypt during the eighteenth and maybe nineteenth dynasties.

Where It's Set: The first fourteen chapters are set in Egypt and northwest Arabia, and the rest on the Sinai Peninsula.

Original Audience: Hebrews—who witnessed a river's water become blood and frogs come out of the waters at God's command and who walked across a parted sea on dry ground while a fire tornado from heaven protected them from Pharaoh's cavalry, but for whatever reason weren't sure they could trust God.

Important Characters: Moses, Pharaoh, Pharaoh's daughter, Aaron, Jethro, Miriam, Joshua.

Type of Book: History narrative, with ancient law and two songs.

Tone and Feel: Epic with the highest stakes.

Story Arc: An underdog story. Moses overcomes problems after hitting rock bottom and leads his people to freedom. In a twist, the Hebrews struggle in their new freedom. They hear straight from God, don't like it, and rebel, but then repent. That cycle repeats through the Old Testament.

Violent Prologue: Exodus opens with Abraham's descendants in slavery. Pharaoh is a jerk who's afraid the Hebrews are too numerous, so he orders that their baby boys be drowned. Moses's mom does not comply. She floats Moses in a basket down the Nile. Pharaoh's daughter finds him and raises him as her own.

Moses Meets God: Years later, Moses kills an Egyptian overseer for cruelty toward a Hebrew slave and flees to the wilderness. There he meets God in a burning bush. God introduces Himself as "I AM" and tells Moses that God will use him to free the Hebrews.

The Plagues and the Exodus: Moses returns to Egypt and confronts Pharaoh, but God hardens Pharaoh's heart. God sends plagues to show His power and that He alone is responsible for saving His people. The extra-important final plague foreshadows Jesus' death on the cross: The firstborn in every Egyptian family dies, but God provides a way out—kill a lamb and put its blood on the doorposts of the house, and the angel of death will pass over.

Pharaoh's spirit is broken. He lets the slaves go.

God compels the Egyptians to heap riches on the departing Hebrews. They head to the desert, but Pharaoh changes his mind and chases them until they're pinned against the sea.

God parts the waters, and they cross on dry ground. Pharaoh's army follows, but the waters close up, and they drown. The Hebrews sing songs to celebrate their freedom.

The Ten Commandments and the Covenant: They travel through the desert to Mount Sinai, where Moses ascends the mountain and God reveals to him the Ten Commandments and the terms of His covenant—basically, "If you obey Me, I'll bless you, but if you disobey Me, I'll punish you. Either way, all nations will know that I am the one true God."

The Disappointing Golden Calf Incident: Down at the foot of the mountain, the Israelites immediately put the terms of the freshly minted covenant to the test by making and worshiping a calf out of the Egyptian gold God gave them. They ignore God's miraculous presence and the miracles they've witnessed. God's not impressed, Moses intervenes, the people are punished, and they repent.

Not Back to Eden, but a Step in the Right Direction: God plans to live among His people—the way it was in the garden of Eden—but it won't be the same. Too much has gone wrong. Sin and its curse haven't been solved yet. So God lives in a tent—a portable temple called the tabernacle. God is holy and perfect. His chosen people are . . . not.

Exodus ends with a problem. God's presence is physically in the tabernacle, but even Moses can't enter because God's glory is too much. The big question is, How can flawed people come into the presence of the flawless God?

Theme: God keeps His promises, delivers His people, and shows Himself to be the one true God.

Important Motifs: Escape from Egypt, manna from heaven in the wilderness, Passover, firstborns, parting water, Sabbath, ascending the mountain to meet God, blood of the covenant, unleavened bread, blood sacrifice, priesthood, the golden calf, the tabernacle. These motifs ripple throughout the rest of the Bible.

Unsung Hero: Moses's wilderness-wife Zipporah and her father, Jethro. They include Moses in their family and support him with their wisdom and keen read on difficult situations Moses encounters.

Saint Catherine's Monastery is located at the base of the traditional site of Mount Sinai (Jebul Musa).
Nicola/stock.adobe.com

Parts You Might Recognize Even If You Haven't Read the Bible: The burning bush, the plagues, crossing the Red Sea, the Ten Commandments, the golden calf.

Stuff You Can Still Physically Look At: This is a bit tricky because there are two proposed dates for when the exodus happened, but there are many ruins from that time, including Pharaoh's palace and the dig sites Tell el-Maskhutah and Qantir that likely correspond to the grain storage cities the Hebrew slaves built (Pithom and Pi-Rameses). Distinctly Hebrew-style homes are unearthed all over Egypt today. Finally, Pharaoh mummies from the era have been exhumed, so you can still look right at the body of someone who was in the Bible.

Most Shocking Moments: The final plague, crossing the Red Sea, and the decision of the freed Hebrews to make and worship a golden calf while God is right there in a miraculous cloud watching what they are doing.

Most Relatable Moment: Moses refuses God's call at the burning bush, claiming he doesn't speak well, but God sends Moses back to Egypt and uses him for good anyway.

Most Applicable Moment for Modern Audiences: God gives the Hebrews good things, but they still act entitled and gripe. It's an easy mistake to make, and it's good that God forgives them.

Most Quoted Moment: The Ten Commandments.

What Would Happen If Exodus Weren't in the Bible? There would be a gigantic plot hole, and the rest of the Old Testament would make zero sense. Exodus introduces Moses, the law, and God's covenant with Moses and explains how the Hebrew people went from slavery to becoming a nation.

Key Verse: Exodus 20:2—"I am the LORD your God, who brought you out of Egypt, out of the land of slavery."

If You Don't Have Time to Read the Whole Thing, at Least Read: The first fifteen chapters for the plagues and Exodus 20 for the Ten Commandments.

When You Visualize Exodus, Picture: The Red Sea parted, with Mount Sinai in the distance.

VITAL STATS

Position: 3 of 66.
Chapters: 27.
Verses: 859.
Word Count: 18,852 (13/66).
Most-Used Words: Lord, offering, priest, shall, altar, blood, unclean (notice "clean" isn't among the most-used words).
Group: The books of Moses.
Also called The Law, The Pentateuch, The Torah, The First Five Books of the Hebrew Bible.
Audience: Ancient Hebrews (and their kids) who escaped Egypt.
Date: Between 1400 and 1200 BC.
Popularity Rank: 33 of 66.

LEVITICUS

Lightning-Fast Summary: Moses and the Israelites have escaped Egypt and God is with them, living in a sacred tent. But God is so holy and glorious that the people can't approach Him. God gives Moses a set of laws for the people to follow so they can be in relationship with Him as a nation.

Unique Feature: All but five of the chapters start with, "The Lord said to Moses . . ." or some variation of that. In total, that phrase appears twenty-eight times. The point seems to be that all this is from God. Moses isn't making it up.

Notice: Sometimes people say Leviticus is the "most boringest" book because it's "just a bunch of outdated rules," but, respectfully, they're wrong. Leviticus has a plot with high stakes. The question of the book is this: Can God still be approached after all that's gone wrong? The answer: There's a big gap between God's holiness and human beings' not-holiness, but yes, the people can still approach God, and here's how.

Who Wrote It? Moses, but God is the author of the law, and this is a book full of the law.

Original Language: Hebrew.

When the Events Happened: As with the other books of Moses, some think it was the last half of the 1400s, while others believe it was the 1200s BC.

Years Covered: Not even one. The whole book happens in about a month.

Historical Setting: Egypt is in one of its golden ages; the Hittites (in modern-day Turkey) are approaching the end of their dominant run, and the land of Canaan (which later becomes Israel) is speckled with mini-city kingdoms, some of which are fierce.

Where It's Set: The Israelite camp near Mount Sinai.

Original Audience: The Hebrews who had come out of slavery in Egypt and the new generation after them who wandered in the desert waiting to muster the courage to take the land God had promised them.

Important Characters: Moses and Aaron.

Type of Book: It's laws—tons of them. But also, weirdly, it's actually a narrative with tons of quotes. These quotes are almost entirely God dictating His laws and instructions to Moses.

Tone and Feel: Dangerous. God comes off as powerful, authoritative, and caring, but not to be trifled with. It is a very serious book.

The Plot: Because God is holy and perfect and the people are not—even Moses—the people are not able to enter the tent where God resides at the end of Exodus. But the first line of Leviticus has God inviting Moses, and only Moses, into the tent. In the first third of the book, God tells Moses how to perform animal sacrifices to Him. In the middle third, God explains how the priesthood will work, and in the last third, God explains the unique moral behavior and rhythms of life He expects from His people.

Theme: God reveals His character and expectations through the law and makes it possible for His people to humbly approach His glory.

Important Motifs: Blood sacrifice, atonement, purification, annual festivals, the priesthood, and most of all, the holiness of God.

Unsung Hero: Aaron, for keeping his composure and continuing to serve God even as he grieved the death of his sons.

Stuff You Can Still Physically Look At: Nothing with certainty. There are theories about the location of Mount Sinai, but no one knows for sure where it is, and since the book only covers one month from more than three thousand years ago, you're going to be hard-pressed to find anything still sitting around out there in the desert.

Most Shocking Moment: God consumes an offering with fire in front of everyone, and right after that, two of Aaron's sons, Nadab and Abihu, are sloppy and flippant with the fire of God, and God consumes them with it.

Most Relatable Moment: The whole assembly waits around, completely dependent on God to spell things out for them. They have no idea how to approach the one true holy God on their own.

Most Applicable Moment for Modern Audiences: For every strange-sounding law in Leviticus, there are ten timeless principles of right relationships with others and with God that are infinitely applicable and useful today.

Most Quoted Moment: Leviticus 19:18—"Do not seek revenge or bear a grudge against anyone among your people, but love your neighbor as yourself. I am the Lord."

What Would Happen If Leviticus Weren't in the Bible? Every time the specifics of the law come up in the rest of the Bible, it wouldn't make sense. If we didn't get all these specifics, we might imagine we could actually uphold the letter and spirit of the law by our own effort.

Key Verse: Leviticus 19:1–2—"The Lord said to Moses, 'Speak to the entire assembly of Israel and say to them: "Be holy because I, the Lord your God, am holy."'"

If You Don't Have Time to Read the Whole Thing, at Least Read: Leviticus 17:11, and also make sure to catch the last verse of the book.

When You Visualize Leviticus, Picture: The law.

VITAL STATS

Position: 4 of 66.
Chapters: 36.
Verses: 1,288.
Word Count: 25,048 (7/66).
Most-Used Words: Lord, offering, son, people, male, tribe, land, clans.
Group: The books of Moses.
Also called The Law, The Pentateuch, The Torah, The First Five Books of the Hebrew Bible.
Audience: Ancient Hebrews (and their kids) who escaped Egypt.
Date: Between 1400 and 1200 BC.
Popularity Rank: 27 of 66.

Lightning-Fast Summary: After a promising start to their lives as a free people under the leadership of the God who freed them, the Israelites lose their way and wander for four decades in the desert. God's already blessed them with lots of people, and shown that He keeps His word, but when God promises them their own land and tells them to go take it, they don't believe Him and waste forty years in the wilderness. As usual, God is faithful anyway, and in the end, a new generation of God's people shows they're ready to go into the promised land.

Unique Feature: Christians don't believe that the man-made English names of the books of the Bible are inspired by God, so it's okay to say that Numbers is a boring, dreadful name that way undersells how dramatic and interesting this book is. The Hebrew title is "In the Wilderness," which sounds cooler and better conveys the point of the book.

Why It's Called Numbers: It has a census at the beginning and another one at the end, after thirty-eight years of wandering in the wilderness. Also, the numbers tell two stories. First, the censuses show there are a lot of Hebrews, meaning that God is keeping His promise to Abraham to make his descendants a great nation. Second, the number of fighting men slightly declines over forty years (from 603,550 to 601,730), which shows how those years were wasted as God's chosen people spun their wheels in the sand out there in the wilderness.

Who Wrote It? Moses.

Years Covered: Thirty-eight long, hard, unnecessary years of wandering in the wilderness.

Historical Setting: In ancient times, before most of the great empires of antiquity had come to be.

Original Language: Hebrew.

Type of Book: A story through and through, but one with abnormally large numbers of statistics woven into the narrative.

Tone and Feel: Senseless and disappointing. The census numbers make it clear there were plenty of fighting men to conquer the promised land, but instead of going into the land, God's people aimlessly wander around and squander an entire generation because of their refusal to trust God. It perks up at the end when the new generation shows they're finally ready to go into the promised land.

Where It's Set: The middle of nowhere between Egypt and Canaan, on and around the Sinai Peninsula.

Stuff You Can Still Physically Look At: Nothing, other than the general landscape of the Sinai Peninsula and the wilderness east of the Jordan River.

Parts You Might Recognize Even If You Haven't Read the Bible: The wilderness wandering or the story of Balaam (the prophet hired to curse Israel but who could only call down blessings on them) and his talking donkey.

Important Characters: Moses, his brother Aaron, their older sister Miriam, Eleazar the priest, Balaam and his donkey, and Joshua, who is heir apparent to Moses as the leader of the Israelites.

At First, Everything Looks Good: The first ten chapters pick up where Leviticus left off at Mount Sinai. Here, God commands Moses to take a census, which reveals that they've got north of 600,000 fighting men and plenty more on top of that to carry out the religious duties of the community. God also spells out more about his relationship with His people. It feels like everything's in place for the Israelites to break camp, march across the wilderness for a couple weeks, and then walk into the promised land, conquering every foe that stands in their way by the power of God.

But then they just sort of don't.

Then the Not-So-Good: Everyone starts complaining along the way. Moses and his family bicker. The unity of the people frays. By the time they get to the edge of the promised land, they're not feeling so confident anymore, and rather than just go in, they decide to send in spies to make sure it's safe. Ten spies come back saying it's too dangerous, and only two come back saying they should trust God and take the land. The crowd goes along with the cowardly spies and then turns on Moses. Without consensus on an action plan, inaction becomes the plan. Their punishment is to meander around in the wilderness for thirty-eight senseless years. The Israelites have to contend with plague, snakes, and rebellion in their camp, and even Moses starts to crack under the pressure and defies God.

In the end, the whole generation that came up out of Egypt but then refused to go into the promised land wanders in the wilderness until they die. Even Moses is denied entry into the land.

Yet in the midst of all of that, God patiently keeps His promises. This is exemplified by a prophet named Balaam who is hired to curse Israel but can't help but bless them by the power of God. Even as the Hebrews complain about Him, God still provides food from heaven to keep them alive in the wilderness. The book ends with the people camped at the doorstep of the promised land, finally ready to act.

Theme: Israel fails their test in the wilderness, but God's redemptive plan persists anyway.

Key Verse: Numbers 14:33–34 (this is God talking in this frightening passage)—"Your children will be shepherds here for forty years, suffering for your unfaithfulness, until the last of your bodies lies in the wilderness. For forty years—one year for each of the forty days you explored the land—you will suffer for your sins and know what it is like to have me against you."

What Would Happen If Numbers Weren't in the Bible? It would seem like the conquest of the promised land was quick and easy and the people conquered it by their good attitudes and hard work. With Numbers in the Bible, we get a vivid contrast between the unfaithfulness of humanity and the faithfulness of God, and we get a preview of how the whole Old Testament is going to play out.

Most Shocking Moment: The earth literally opens up and swallows the people who complained the hardest at Moses.

Important Motifs: Wilderness, desert, milk and honey, cloud and flame, God's presence, sprinkling water for purification, and the bronze snake, which was set up to miraculously heal anyone who was bit by the camp vipers.

Unsung Hero: They're actually pretty well-sung, but we're going with Joshua and Caleb, who were the only two spies to trust God and give a hopeful report about going into the land.

Most Relatable Moment: Everyone complaining and turning on each other because of the conditions on a long trip.

Most Quoted Moment: The priestly blessing in Numbers 6:24–26—"The Lord bless you and keep you; the Lord make his face shine on you and be gracious to you; the Lord turn his face toward you and give you peace."

Most Applicable Moment For Modern Audiences: The disbelieving old generation wants to wander, and God eventually gives them what they want. When a new generation comes along that trusts God and wants to follow Him, He gives them what they want as well.

If You Don't Have Time to Read the Whole Thing, at Least Read: The story of Balaam in Numbers 23 and 24; read also Numbers 14, which is the key to the book and quoted in Psalm 95 and Hebrews 3.

When You Visualize Numbers, Picture: Wilderness wandering.

VITAL STATS

Position: 5 of 66.
Chapters: 34.
Verses: 959.
Word Count: 23,008 (8/66).
Most-Used Words: Lord, God, land, giving, today, eat.
Group: The books of Moses.
Also called The Law, The Pentateuch, The Torah, The First Five Books of the Hebrew Bible.
Audience: Ancient Hebrews (and their kids) who escaped Egypt.
Date: Between 1400 and 1200 BC.
Popularity Rank: 19 of 66.

Lightning-Fast Summary: The generation of Israelites who refused to go into the promised land are all nearly dead, and a new generation stands ready to trust God and follow Him into Canaan. Before they go, Moses reminds them of who their God is by laying out the law and renewing their covenant with God.

Unique Feature: The name communicates the idea of a second giving of the law. Deuteronomy covers the same law from earlier in the Bible, but this time it's being read to a new and younger audience.

Original Name: The Hebrew title is just the first phrase of the book, which is "These Are the Words."

Who Wrote It? Moses (except for the little bit at the end after Moses dies).

When It Was Written and When the Events Happened: Moses wrote this at the end of his life, about things that happened near the end of his life, somewhere between the 1400s and 1200s BC.

Years Covered: Less than one. Probably only a couple months.

Historical Setting: A few weeks before the kingdoms and tribes of Canaan would be conquered by the Israelites.

Original Language: Hebrew.

Original Audience: The up-and-coming generation of Israelites who had been born during the four decades of wilderness wandering and were now poised to take the land God had promised.

Type of Book: Technically a narrative, but almost the whole book is Moses addressing the Israelites, with big chunks of law embedded throughout.

Tone and Feel: Compared to Numbers, this book feels freshly infused with youth and optimism.

Where It's Set: In Moab, just east of the Dead Sea.

Stuff You Can Still Physically Look At: You can stand on Mount Nebo in modern-day Jordan and look west into the promised land from the same vantage point Moses had before he died.

Parts You Might Recognize Even If You Haven't Read the Bible: The Ten Commandments make a second appearance in Deuteronomy 5 (they originally appeared in Exodus 20), and there's a famous prayer in Deuteronomy 6 called the *Shema*.

Important Characters: Moses, Joshua, and the up-and-coming generation that will go into the promised land soon.

Fighting Words, Then Parting Words: The book opens with a few military conquests that have the Israelites positioned to finally move into the promised land, but rather than charge ahead (the conquest unfolds in the next book), there is a lull in the action. Moses isn't going to enter the land. God has ordained that he'll die in the wilderness. But before that happens, Moses musters all he has left to spell out the law to the new generation and to make sure the covenant between them and God is understood and renewed. Moses sees to it that they know there is only one God, and that they are to worship no others. God is their God and they are His people, and God is going to make that obvious to the whole world through this relationship. If they obey Him, God will bless them, and if they disobey Him, God will punish them. Either way, everyone will know He is the one true God and they are His people. The people agree to that.

Moses Dies: It's bittersweet to see the end of Moses's part of the story. He cares about the future of his people and does everything he can to ensure they'll get it right, even though he knows he'll never set foot in the promised land. Moses hands off leadership to Joshua, son of Nun (one of the two spies who gave positive reports in Numbers), and then the book ends on Mount Nebo with Moses closing his eyes for the last time after looking toward the land God promised His people.

Theme: Israel is God's chosen people, and they've got a lasting covenant together. If they obey Him, He'll bless them, and if they disobey Him, He'll punish them. Either way, everyone will know that He is the one true God and they are His people.

Key Verses: The *Shema* in Deuteronomy 6:4–5—"Hear, O Israel: The LORD our God, the LORD is one. Love the LORD your God with all your heart and with all your soul and with all your strength."

Bonus Key Verses: Deuteronomy 30:19–20, which kind of sums up the whole point of the book—"This day I call the heavens and the earth as witnesses against you that I have set before you life and death, blessings and curses. Now choose life, so that you and your children may live and that you may love the LORD your God, listen to his voice, and hold fast to him. For the LORD is your life, and he will give you many years in the land he swore to give to your fathers, Abraham, Isaac and Jacob."

Another Bonus Key Verse: Deuteronomy 30:4, where God promises—"Even if you have been banished to the most distant land under the heavens, from there the LORD your God will gather you and bring you back." This promise has huge implications a thousand years later in the Old Testament when God's people are banished but try to pull it back together and obey God during the time of Ezra and Nehemiah. Nehemiah basically prays this verse back to God to remind Him of this promise (Nehemiah 1:8–9).

Where Deuteronomy Fits in the Larger Bible: Deuteronomy is the connective tissue between the super-ancient Torah and the rest of the Bible moving forward. It sums up the Torah and springboards the reader into the way things are going to be for the rest of the Old Testament.

Most Shocking Moment: Right before Moses leaves the camp for the last time, he tenderly recites to the people a song he wrote that sums up everything.

Later Bible Payoff: When Jesus is at the end of His time in the wilderness in Matthew 4, He quotes from Deuteronomy three times, which is cool because Deuteronomy is the book that covers the end of the wilderness time in the Old Testament.

Unsung Heroes: Those from the next generation of Israelites who eagerly learned from Moses and, like Abraham, believed God.

Most Relatable Moment: Moses contending with his mortality.

Most Quoted Moment: The *Shema* (Deuteronomy 6:4–5, quoted on previous page)—Jesus Himself quotes it in Mark 12:28–30.

If You Don't Have Time to Read the Whole Thing, at Least Read: The *Shema* in context in Deuteronomy 6 and the Song of Moses in Deuteronomy 32.

When You Visualize Deuteronomy, Picture: Old Moses passing the baton to Joshua and the kids.

Looking west toward the promised land from the top of Mount Nebo.

Emanuele Mazzoni/Getty Images

VITAL STATS

Position: 6 of 66.
Chapters: 24.
Verses: 658.
Word Count: 15,671 (19/66).
Most-Used Words: Lord, Joshua, Israel, land, king, towns, Jordan, people.
Group: Old Testament history.
Audience: Hebrews who conquered Canaan, and their descendants.
Date: 1400ish BC, but maybe 1200ish.
Popularity Rank: 30 of 66.

JOSHUA

Lightning-Fast Summary: Joshua becomes leader of the Israelites after Moses dies, and he leads them to conquer the land God promised them. God rightly gets credit. Israel promises to remember that and obey Him forever.

Unique Feature: The phrase "to this very day" pops up throughout the book to show that the conquest had (and would continue) to stand the test of time.

Two Big Things: Conquest and covenant. The first two-thirds covers the conquest part, and the last third speaks to remembering and renewing the covenant.

Elephant in the Room: This book has a ton of war and killing in it, and the author treats it like this is a very good thing commanded by God Himself. This feels foreign and conflicting to many modern readers, but this ancient conquest account doesn't apologize for the victories on the battlefield at all. Rather, the book treats this story as God doing three things at once:

1. Judging a vile people group and bringing justice for all the people they wronged
2. Blessing the descendants of Abraham as He promised He would

3. Advancing His Bible-wide redemptive plan by establishing His people in the land

Who Wrote It? We don't know (but Joshua probably contributed to some parts).

Years Covered: Around thirty.

When the Events Happened: Probably from the late 1400s BC to the 1370s BC, but some smart people put it after 1250 BC.

Historical Setting: There was a big shakeup in the ancient world when economies, societies, and boundaries all changed quickly, and what happens in Joshua looks like it was part of that shakeup.

When It Was Written: Mostly during the time in which it's set, but there are a few comments here and there about landmarks and memory that hint at the book of Joshua reaching its final form many generations later. Christians believe all of it is inspired by God.

Original Language: Hebrew.

Original Audience: Hebrews living in the promised land after the conquest who could still see monuments from the conquest "to this very day."

Type of Book: It's a military history meant to explain and justify the land boundaries and ownership at the time it was written, but it's also a theology book that gives God credit for the conquest and demands that readers continue to obey Him.

Tone and Feel: Triumphant! After a lot of wandering and delays, it's finally time to take the land God promised the people. Joshua unapologetically celebrates the God-ordained conquest of Canaan.

Where It's Set: Almost entirely in modern-day Israel, with a little bit of Jordan, Syria, and Lebanon.

Stuff You Can Still Physically Look At: There's still a city of Jericho and a dig site right next to it called Tell es-Sultan. It's a UNESCO World Heritage site, and it's got layers of ruins and walls dating back thousands of years, including a burn layer from a catastrophe that dates roughly to the time of Joshua.

Parts You Might Recognize Even If You Haven't Read the Bible: The battle of Jericho, where the Israelites marched around the city playing music, and then God miraculously knocked down the walls.

Important Characters: The three main characters are God, Joshua, and the people of Israel collectively. Other important characters include Eleazar and Phinehas the priests, Caleb, Achan, and a Canaanite prostitute named Rahab (that's how she's known to history, but she's great, and Joshua spares her and her family when he conquers Jericho).

Conquest: Moses and the generation that miraculously escaped from Egypt accomplished little in their forty years of wandering in the wilderness, but they did manage to defeat the tribes and kingdoms east of the promised land and establish a secure staging area for their invasion of Canaan. After Moses dies, Joshua is installed as leader, and he guides the people across the Jordan River to Jericho—a walled stronghold city that was ancient even to the ancients. The Israelites cannot conquer the land without taking Jericho—a nearly impossible feat from a conventional military perspective. The city is just too well provisioned and well fortified. But God miraculously knocks down thick city walls, and the city falls to Joshua. With this one miraculous act, God made it clear that no one can oppose His power. There are bumps along the way, but from here on out, the conquest is a foregone conclusion.

Remembering and Renewing the Covenant: In the final seven chapters of the book, Joshua allots the conquered land to the tribes of Israel and again renews the covenant between God and Israel (that's the third time). Joshua assertively challenges the people to be faithful to the covenant and to obey and worship God alone. They all say they agree, but Joshua seems skeptical.

The book ends with the death and burial of Joshua and with parts of the land God commanded Israel to conquer left untaken.

That last thing is going to be a big issue moving forward.

Theme: God kept His promises by providing the land. Israel is supposed to remember that, honor the covenant, and obey God.

Key Verse for the First Part (the Conquest): Joshua 1:6 (God talking to Joshua)—"Be strong and courageous, because you will lead these people to inherit the land I swore to their ancestors to give them."

Key Verse for the Second Part (the Covenant): Joshua 24:15 (Joshua talking to the people)—"But if serving the LORD seems undesirable to you, then choose for yourselves this day whom you will serve, whether the gods your ancestors served beyond the Euphrates, or the gods of the Amorites, in whose land you are living. But as for me and my household, we will serve the Lord."

What Would Happen If Joshua Weren't in the Bible? It would look like the Bible was trying to whitewash the conquest. Instead, the Bible acknowledges that God used war as a tool of judgment, justice, and blessing. It's better for the reader to wrestle with these stories than for the Bible to duck them.

Where Joshua Fits in the Larger Bible: At this point in history, time was up for nomadic people groups in that part of the world. They either had to find a land and put down roots or get absorbed into cultures that had established their land. Nomads who couldn't find a home were lost to history. The clock was ticking for the Israelites, who'd been slaves and nomads for a thousand years, and in Joshua, we finally see them escape from that transience, which would have a been a cultural-historical death sentence if it had gone on much longer.

Most Shocking Moment: Joshua is in the middle of a battle that's going well, so he prays to God to stop the sun in its place so he can finish off the enemy. Whether the sun literally held firm in the sky or some other light-giving astronomical event happened at just that moment, the event serves as confirmation that this wasn't just another squabble between ancient Near Eastern tribes, but was rather the miraculous plan of God.

Important Motifs: God-ordained total victory, the Jordan River, the twelve tribes of Israel, the promised land, remembrance, and God's covenants with His people.

Unsung Hero: Phinehas (the priest) and the leaders of most of the other tribes, who calmly listen to the leaders of the tribes of Reuben, Gad, and Manasseh so as to avoid a tragic civil war over a misunderstanding in Joshua 22.

Most Quoted Moment: Joshua 24:15 (quoted on previous page)—this is a great verse about being faithful to God even when it isn't popular or easy. It's understandably the sort of verse you see in living room art and tattoos.

If You Don't Have Time to Read the Whole Thing, at Least Read: Joshua 6 to get the Jericho story and Joshua 24 for the renewal of the covenant.

When You Visualize Joshua, Picture: Jericho's walls falling down and battle-hardened Joshua leading the covenant renewal at the end of his life.

Excavations at tel Jericho, said to be the oldest fortified city in the world.

Robert Hoetink/stock.adobe.com

VITAL STATS

Position: 7 of 66.
Chapters: 21.
Verses: 618.
Word Count: 15,385 (21/66).
Most-Used Words: Lord, men, Israel, God, people, son, man.
Group: Old Testament history.
Audience: Israelites who needed to remember the era of the judges.
Date: Around 1000 BC.
Popularity Rank: 40 of 66.

JUDGES

Lightning-Fast Summary: Israel has mostly conquered the promised land, but after a few years, the new generation disobeys God, and an age of chaos ensues. They don't have a king or kingdom to fight off oppressors, but after enough hardship, the people call out to God, and He sends liberators to save them.

Unique Feature #1: Judges were leaders of varying moral quality sent by God to deliver Israel from their enemies. The book of Judges is about the era of their on-again, off-again leadership in the time between the conquest of the promised land and the beginning of the united kingdom of Israel.

Unique Feature #2: The judges seem like the heroes of the book, but they're super flawed. At times they're cowardly, dishonest, selfish, violent for no reason, stupidly shortsighted, and rash. Some seem to completely misunderstand the character of God and behave like He is a petty Canaanite pagan god. They do heroic things by the power of God but mostly lack heroic character.

Unique Feature #3: Reading this book feels like being caught in a whirlpool. The seemingly inescapable cycle is sad and tiring, but that's the central point: Left to their own ends, the people will be forgetful and disobedient. They have centuries to create a leaderless, God-honoring society but fail miserably.

When the Events Happened: From the end of Joshua's life in the 1380s BC through the run-up to the kingdom of Israel in the mid-1000s BC.

Time Covered: A lot. This isn't a little blip on the timeline. The chaotic age of the judges lasted much longer than the current age of the United States.

Key Verse: The very last verse of the book sums up the whole thing: Judges 21:25—"In those days Israel had no king; everyone did as they saw fit."

Structure: The story is shaped like a bunch of circles drawn roughly over the top of each other. The cycle goes like this:

1. Israel is fat and happy and forgets God and disobeys.
2. God gives them over to oppressors (the text makes it clear it is God who does this).
3. Israel goes through hard times, which makes them remember God and ask for His help.
4. God gives them a judge, who defeats the oppressor.
5. There's peace in Israel, which makes everybody fat and happy.
6. Being fat and happy makes everyone forget about God.
7. Repeat.

Who Wrote It? We don't know, but whoever it was wasn't impressed with this era.

Historical Setting: This was a time when the ancient superpowers weren't the most super. Because there was no threatening nation looming over Israel, lots of little regional kingdoms pop up and become a nuisance. They oppress Israel for a few decades and then fade away again.

Original Language: Hebrew.

Original Audience: Israelites living in their relatively recently founded kingdom who might still have a bit of living memory of the era of the judges.

Type of Book: Cautionary history.

Tone and Feel: Tragic and filled with stories of squandered potential and missing the point.

Where It's Set: In Israel and the little surrounding kingdoms.

Stuff You Can Still Physically Look At: There are several archaeological sites that seem to match descriptions of towns in Judges, including a site near Jericho that might correspond to the palace of Eglon, who was famously stabbed in his fat belly by Ehud, the left-handed judge.

Parts You Might Recognize Even If You Haven't Read the Bible: The story of Samson and Delilah.

Important Characters: The people of Israel, the neighboring peoples, Eglon the king of Moab, Ehud, Sisera, Jael, Deborah, Barak, Gideon, Jephthah, Samson, and Delilah.

Things Go Off the Rails After Joshua: While Joshua is alive, Israel remembers what God has done for them and mostly obeys Him, but they never completely conquer the land as instructed, and that comes back to bite them in the butt throughout Judges and the rest of the Old Testament. After Joshua dies, a new generation comes along that doesn't care about obeying God.

Flawed Judges Barely Hold Things Together: This new generation is attracted to the cultures and religions of the people they never fully conquered. God acts in keeping with the covenant He made with Israel and Moses, which Joshua also reaffirms, and punishes His people using corrupt foreign kingdoms like those of the Moabites, Midianites, Ammonites, and Philistines. After things get bad enough, the Israelites remember God and beg for His help. Then God gives them judges to throw off the oppressors, even though some of the judges use their power in weird and destructive ways. The book ends with a horrible civil war in which all of Israel attacks the tribe of Benjamin after a gruesome incident involving a mutilated concubine.

When it's all over, it doesn't feel like the people of Israel, or God's redemptive plan, have progressed.

But Here's the Vague Silver Lining of Judges: God gave the Israelites (and humanity in general) a long leash in Judges, and it did not go well. After this era, there's no doubt that humanity is incapable of solving its own problems. This points the reader back to dependence on God and eventually to Jesus.

Theme: Humanity is a busted-up mess and in need of a good king. Godly human kings can help make it better, but ultimately the only real hope is found in God's kingdom.

What Would Happen If Judges Weren't in the Bible? We'd have no explanation for why the tribes of Israel would voluntarily give up their autonomy and submit to a king. Also, we find out in Judges that anarchy can't break the curse. In the next few books, we'll see that human authoritarianism can't break it either.

Most Shocking Moments: Judges probably has the highest shocking-moments-per-page ratio in the whole Bible. Here are three:

1. Ehud the judge assassinated Eglon the king of Moab by plunging a sword so far into his fat that the king poops himself.
2. Jael invites the wicked general Sisera into her tent. He and his king have oppressed Israel for twenty years, but now he's vulnerable and on the run. She puts him to sleep with warm milk, then pounds a tent peg through his brain.
3. Jephthah the judge misunderstands the character of God so much that he makes a rash vow to sacrifice to God the first thing that runs out of his house to meet him when he returns home. His daughter comes to him first, and Jephthah follows through on his ill-advised oath.

Refreshing Part: There's a prophetess named Deborah, who holds court under a palm tree because no one else is providing any leadership to the people. She's an effective leader and probably the least compromised of all the judges. In Judges 4, she defeats the Canaanites with the reluctant help of Barak, and then in Judges 5, she sings a victory song.

Unsung Hero: The unmentioned minority of Israelites who must have quietly persevered in faith when it was unpopular to do so.

If You Don't Have Time to Read the Whole Thing, at Least Read: The Samson story in chapters 13–16.

When You Visualize Judges, Picture: Samson collapsing the temple on his enemies and himself.

Temple ruins, Ashkelon

v_blinov/stock.adobe.com

VITAL STATS

Position: 8 of 66.

Chapters: 4.

Verses: 85.

Word Count: 2,039 (43/66).

Most-Used Words: Law, father, daughter, mother.

Group: Old Testament history.

Audience: Israel.

Date: About 1000 BC.

Popularity Rank: 53 of 66.

Lightning-Fast Summary: Set against the bleak backdrop of the era of the judges, Ruth tells the story of a young Gentile widow who faithfully follows Naomi (her Jewish mother-in-law) back to her home in Bethlehem. There Ruth meets a man of character named Boaz, and they get married. Through all this, Naomi, who lost everything, has her fortunes reversed.

Unique Feature: Ruth is a beautiful ancient love story that would be a classic even if it had no larger point. But what makes it even better is the fact that Ruth and Boaz turn out to be the great-grandparents of King David. This book is great as a love story, as a backstory, and as a story of God's faithfulness in the midst of ugly times.

When the Events Happened: During the era of the judges, probably in the 1100s BC.

When It Was Written: During the reign of David, maybe around 1000 BC.

Time Covered: The book concludes with a genealogy that looks forward and backward a few generations, but the story itself covers a comparatively short amount of time.

Who Wrote It? We have no idea.

Key Verse: Ruth refuses to leave her mother-in-law, Naomi, in Ruth 1:16—"But Ruth replied, 'Don't urge me to leave you or to turn back from you. Where you go I will go, and where you stay I will stay. Your people will be my people and your God my God.'"

Structure: Ruth is ruthlessly symmetrical. It opens with a problem, then has four storytelling acts of matching lengths, and concludes with the solution to the problem. The pivot point of the story is exactly in the middle of the book (2:20).

Historical Setting: During and after a nasty famine during the era of the judges.

Original Language: Hebrew.

Original Audience: Israelites living in their relatively recently founded kingdom who might still have a bit of living memory of the era of the judges.

Type of Book: Family history.

Tone and Feel: Warm, tender, and with much smaller stakes than anything we've seen so far in the Bible.

Where It's Set: Moab for the first little bit, and then the majority is in Bethlehem, where David and Jesus were later born.

Stuff You Can Still Physically Look At: The town of Bethlehem is still there, but there's not much to see from the super-ancient world of Ruth and Boaz.

Important Characters: Naomi, Orpah, Ruth, Boaz, Elimelek, an unnamed relative of Elimelek, and David.

A Story of Love and Redemption: Elimelek and his wife, Naomi, move with their two sons from their home in Bethlehem to the land of Moab to escape a famine. Elimelek dies, and the sons later marry Moabite women, but then the sons both die as well. Naomi is left with nothing and decides to return home to Bethlehem. One daughter-in-law stays in Moab, but the other, Ruth, won't leave Naomi and moves to Bethlehem with her.

There Ruth catches the eye of a good and prominent man named Boaz. It seems like they're destined to be together, but there's a catch. The law says a certain relative of Elimelek is entitled to marry Ruth to help restore what's left of the household and lineage of Elimelek. However, that relative declines the obligation and gives Boaz and Ruth his blessing. They get married and have a son named Obed, and Naomi, who in many ways is the female version of Job in the Bible, is restored.

Ruth's Legacy: At the very end of the book, one more good thing is cleverly revealed: It turns out that Obed would go on to have a son named Jesse, and that Jesse would go on to be the father of the great King David. What seemed like just a sweet story of love and redemption turns out to play a key role in the origin story of King David as well.

Theme: God uses the faithfulness of Ruth and Boaz to redeem a widow who lost everything (Naomi), and in doing so, He moves forward His redemptive plan for everyone.

Kinsman-Redeemer: This is the role the unnamed relative declined and Boaz accepted. It looked like the line of Naomi's family would be snuffed out because of the deaths of her husband and sons in Moab, but then Boaz stepped in to redeem and reverse the tragedy at his own expense because of his own character. This is reflective of the character of God and the work of Jesus later in the Bible.

What Would Happen If Ruth Weren't in the Bible? The story would hang together just fine. There are other accounts of David's genealogy and other examples of God caring for people in desperate need. But Ruth is a drink of cool water when you're reading straight through the Bible. Everything up to this point has been *very* high stakes and often bleak, and nothing has been bleaker than the era of the judges. Then along comes Ruth. We take a break to focus in on one of the bajillions of ancient Near Eastern widows who ever lived (nearly all of whom are completely forgotten), and we see in her suffering and in her triumph that God working out her story is also God working out the grand redemptive story of the whole Bible.

Most Shocking Moment: When Ruth refuses to abandon her mother-in-law.

Unsung Hero: Elimelek, for doing something difficult to protect his family during hard times, even though it ended up costing him.

If You Don't Have Time to Read the Whole Thing, at Least Read: Don't be like that. Just read all four chapters. You'll love it.

When You Visualize Ruth, Picture: Boaz spreading the corner of his garment over Ruth.

1 & 2 SAMUEL

VITAL STATS

Position: 9 and 10 of 66.
Chapters: 55.
Verses: 1,505.
Word Count: 20,837 and 17,170 (10/66 and 17/66).
Most-Used Words: Lord, God, Saul, David, man, Samuel, Israel, Philistines, king, son, words, earth, eyes.
Group: Old Testament history.
Audience: Israel.
Date: Between 931 BC and 722 BC.
Popularity Rank: 21 and 37 of 66.

Lightning-Fast Summary: These books tell the story of how Israel emerged from the era of the judges and got a king . . . and also why they maybe shouldn't have. They tell the story of the run-up to Israel becoming a kingdom and then chronicle the reigns of King Saul and King David.

Unique Feature: First and Second Samuel were originally one book, but the guys who translated the Old Testament from Hebrew into Greek split it into two parts a couple hundred years before Jesus.

The translators were smart and put the break at the perfect place to have it all make sense as two separate, cohesive stories.

Part 1 focuses on the prophet Samuel and the reign of King Saul.

Part 2 follows the reign of King David.

Big Book: First and Second Samuel combined make up over 6 percent of the Bible.

Who Wrote It? Probably a group project. Samuel (and Chronicles) reference a handful of books that are no longer around that the author or editor of Samuel was using.

The prophet Samuel might have written parts of the book, but he definitely didn't write 2 Samuel because he dies at the end of 1 Samuel.

When It Was Written: Sometime after Solomon's reign (he died in 931 BC) but before Assyria conquered the Northern Kingdom of Israel in 722 BC.

When the Events Happened: It starts at the end of the era of the judges and runs up to just before King David dies in 970 BC.

Years Covered: Around 130 years—all of the 1000s and little bit of the 900s BC.

Original Language: Hebrew.

Original Audience: The Israelites, who needed to know the history of their monarchy and God's role in it.

Type of Book: Royal history / national history.

Tone and Feel: Action-packed with complex characters. There's a sense of foreboding as Saul gradually spirals toward tragic failure, but David provides a glimmer of hope throughout.

Where It's Set: All around Israel, with quick visits to Moab and Philistia.

Stuff You Can Still Physically Look At: There's a lot of named geography you can easily visit, like the Valley of Elah, where David and Goliath fought in 1 Samuel 17, or the caves of En Gedi (now a national park), where David cut a corner from King Saul's robe in 1 Samuel 24. Ruins of lots of cities, including part of Jerusalem built by David, still dot the landscape of Israel to this day.

Parts You Might Recognize Even If You Haven't Read the Bible: David and Goliath, David's friendship with Jonathan, the story of David and Bathsheba.

Important Characters: The book is named for Samuel because he's a prophet, the last of the judges, and the guy who formed the monarchy. That said, David is the main character in these books, with Saul and his son Jonathan playing important roles as well. Other key characters include Hannah, Goliath, Abigail, the witch of Endor, Abner, Joab, Ish-Bosheth, Nathan the prophet, Bathsheba, Uriah the Hittite, Tamar, Absalom, David's mighty warriors, and Solomon.

Story Arc: King Saul rises to power, wobbles, then spirals, and ultimately fails the test. King David rises to power, wobbles, repents, then recovers, and ultimately passes the test with tons of God's help.

Prologue: Things have been mostly awful for nearly three hundred years during the age of the judges, but the tender little story of Ruth shows there were also redemptive things happening if one looked closely enough. First Samuel opens with the story of another faithful woman named Hannah, who is finally given a son after years of childlessness. She names him Samuel and dedicates him to the service of the Lord after he's weaned. She brings Samuel to the house of the Lord to live with and learn from Eli, the priest. Samuel turns out to be a great prophet and the last of the judges all at once. During this time, the Israelites face their most challenging oppressor to date—the Philistines.

We Want a King Just Like Everybody Else: In the midst of this, the people, who are understandably tired of the roller-coaster ride that defined the era of the judges, go to Samuel to demand a king. Samuel warns them about kings, but the people won't hear it. So Samuel anoints Saul as king. Saul is decent at first, but the job takes a toll on him, and his darker character traits gradually begin to manifest. Samuel warns him, but Saul keeps getting it wrong. Eventually God rejects Saul as king, and Samuel seeks out God's choice for who is next in line.

Saul's Slide into Suicide: Samuel finds young David from the household of Jesse and anoints him as king. From there, David's fame only grows when he miraculously defeats the Philistine giant Goliath, which turns the tide of the whole Israel-Philistine war. Saul is jealous and tries to kill David in the palace, but Prince Jonathan helps David escape. Saul hunts David all over Israel. David has chances to kill Saul but won't do it. Saul has moments of apparent repentance, but his pride always wins out, and eventually Saul takes his own life after being wounded in battle by the Philistines.

That's where the break between 1 and 2 Samuel happens.

King David Sits on the Throne: In part 2, David finds out that Saul and Jonathan are dead, and he mourns for them. After that, David still has to fight what's left of Saul's household to secure the kingdom, but he wins and becomes king over all of Israel. David then conquers Jerusalem, makes it his capital, and decides to build a great temple for God to live in there.

This next part is very important!

Jesus Will Reign on David's Throne Forever: God tells David through the prophet Nathan that God is going to establish David's throne forever. As we read along in the Bible, it becomes more and more clear that the One who will reign on David's throne forever is none other than Jesus. The book of Matthew particularly spells this out.

Like God's promise to Abraham in the book of Genesis, this is an unconditional promise. God says He will keep His word, even if David does stupid things.

And stupid things David does.

David Fails and Recovers: David defeats the Moabites, the Philistines, and the Ammonites, but with those battles won, David turns his attention to another man's wife. He gets Bathsheba pregnant and eventually has Joab (his military commander) leave Bathsheba's husband alone to die in the heat of battle. God is unimpressed. David repents yet still suffers the consequences of his sin. God spares David, but the seeds of family chaos have been sewn, and David's own sons rebel against him in overt and sneaky ways.

At the end of 1 and 2 Samuel, the reign of David has some black eyes, but taking everything into consideration, he's had a good reign and has ruled as a flawed man who is quick to repent—a man after God's own heart.

Theme: God opposes the proud but shows favor to the humble.

Important Motifs: The ark of the covenant, God raising up and taking down rulers, kingship, the idea of a coming Messiah.

Key Verse #1: 1 Samuel 8:5 (this is the people confronting Samuel)—"They said to him, 'You are old, and your sons do not follow your ways; now appoint a king to lead us, such as all the other nations have.'"

Key Verse #2: 2 Samuel 7:16 (this is God making a promise to David)—"Your house and your kingdom will endure forever before me; your throne will be established forever."

Most Quoted Moment: 1 Samuel 16:7, when Samuel is picking who God wants to be the next king—"But the LORD said to Samuel, 'Do not consider his appearance or his height, for I have rejected him. The LORD does not look at the things people look at. People look at the outward appearance, but the LORD looks at the heart.'"

What Would Happen If 1 and 2 Samuel Weren't in the Bible? We'd be missing the answers to two really important questions that have to be tackled for the Bible to make sense.

1. How did Israel go from being a confederation of chaotic tribes ruled intermittently by equally chaotic judges to becoming a lasting kingdom?
2. Is God still planning to redeem humanity through these people after all that's happened?

Most Shocking Moment: A young teenage boy kills the greatest warrior on earth in front of everyone with a sling and a rock. This story is so famous it's the most popular metaphor in history for an underdog winning against all odds.

Unsung Heroes: Ruth (even though she isn't in the book) and Hannah. Two suffering yet faithful women whose decisions brought about the best judge (Samuel) and the best king (David) in the history of Israel.

Most Relatable Moment: The prophet Nathan comes to confront David about his sin, but David gets on his indignant high horse because he doesn't realize that Nathan is talking about him. Then David looks like an idiot and experiences a rush of humiliation, grief, and regret over his mistakes.

Most Controversial Part: King Saul shows mercy and spares the defeated King Agag, even though God told him not to, and then God rejects Saul as king because of it.

Most Applicable Moment for Modern Audiences: When Jonathan has to choose between helping his best friend survive and honoring his dad's wish to see David killed. Jonathan did the right thing, even though it was very hard and very costly.

If You Don't Have Time to Read the Whole Thing, at Least Read: Hannah's song in 1 Samuel 2, and God's covenant with David in 2 Samuel 7.

When You Visualize 1 and 2 Samuel, Picture: Samuel anointing Saul and then David, David and Goliath, and David on a throne that God promised would become eternal.

Excavations at the City of David.

Kira/stock.adobe.com

1 & 2 KINGS

VITAL STATS

Position: 11 and 12 of 66.
Chapters: 47.
Verses: 1,535.
Word Count: 20,361 and 18,784 (11/66 and 14/66).
Most-Used Words: Lord, king, Israel, Solomon, son, Judah, God, temple, David, Elisha.
Group: Old Testament history.
Audience: Exiled Jews.
Date: After 586 BC.
Popularity Rank: 34 and 38 of 66.

Lightning-Fast Summary: The story of all the kings of Israel and Judah other than Saul and David. It starts with the golden age of King Solomon, but then the kingdom splits in two—Israel and Judah—and most of the kings after that aren't great. Eventually both kingdoms get conquered by foreign empires.

Unique Feature: First and Second Kings were originally one book but got split up a couple hundred years before Jesus. If they were still together, Kings would be the longest book in the Bible. First and Second Kings account for 6.5 percent of the total word count of the Bible.

Years Covered: About 400. Other than the reigns of Saul and David, Kings covers the whole history of the Israelite kingdoms from beginning to end, naming every king from the 970s BC to the last of them in the 580s BC.

Who Wrote It? Nobody knows, but Jewish tradition says Jeremiah.

When It Was Written: Whoever wrote it saw Jerusalem conquered by Nebuchadnezzar and the Babylonians in 586 BC, so it had to be after that.

Original Language: Hebrew, but it was translated into ancient Greek in the 200s BC.

Original Audience: Jews living as exiles in Babylon who were looking back on the collapse of their kingdom and trying to make sense of what happened.

Type of Book: Tragic history and theological cautionary tale.

Tone and Feel: A well-deserved scolding over the stupidity of a calamity unfolding in slow motion over the course of forty-seven mostly agonizing chapters.

Where It's Set: Israel (the Northern Kingdom) and Judah (the Southern Kingdom), with a quick dip into Babylon right at the end.

One Cool Thing You Can Still Physically Look At: The Assyrians laid siege to the Israelite city of Lachish in 2 Kings 18. You can still go to the site and see their siege ramp. The British Museum has a relief taken from Nineveh that portrays the siege from the Assyrian perspective.

Parts You Might Recognize Even If You Haven't Read the Bible: Solomon suggesting cutting a baby in half to resolve a dispute between two women over who was the baby's real mom. First Kings tells of the hijinks of the scoundrel King Ahab and the wicked Queen Jezebel.

Important Characters:

Prophets: Elijah, Elisha (his successor), Jonah, Micaiah, and Isaiah.

Kings: Solomon, Jeroboam, Rehoboam, Ahab (and his wife Jezebel), Hezekiah, Jehoshaphat, Manasseh, and Josiah, who rediscovered the Book of the Law and brought the people back to the worship of God.

Foreign Kings: Nebuchadnezzar of Babylon (who conquered Judah), Pharaoh Shishak of Egypt, Ben-Hadad of Aram, and Tiglath-Pileser and Sennacherib of Assyria.

Solomon and His Temple: King David dies in 1 Kings 2, and Solomon comes to power. Solomon isn't perfect, but he's blessed with exceptional wisdom and rules over the golden age of the kingdom of Israel. During that time, he builds the temple and throws an extravagant dedication ceremony. At that event, the presence of God appears in the form of a dark cloud and takes up residence in the temple. You'd think that would be enough to keep future generations enthusiastic about serving God, but you'd be wrong.

The Kingdom Splits in Two: Solomon flounders in his dedication to God in his later years, and his sons Jeroboam and Rehoboam fumblingly divide their father's kingdom in two. Roughly ten tribes descended from Abraham and Jacob go north and become the kingdom of Israel, their capital eventually landing in Samaria. Two tribes, Judah and Benjamin (along with descendants of Levi), become the kingdom of Judah and have their capital in Jerusalem.

The Northern Kingdom Is a Dumpster Fire: The North produces no good kings and is constantly palling around with fake local gods. King Ahab and his wife Jezebel are the worst of the bunch, and the prophet Elijah arises to challenge them. He has a showdown with Ahab's prophets (who worship a Canaanite deity called Baal). Long story short: God shows up, Baal doesn't. Elijah relentlessly mocks Baal's prophets the whole time. God looks great, and Ahab, Jezebel, and Baal (along with his prophets) come out looking like idiots. First Kings ends with Elijah's prophecies of doom against Ahab and Jezebel coming to pass.

The Fall of the North: Second Kings opens with Elijah passing his authority to a successor prophet named Elisha. This handoff of authority is clear and clean and stands in stark contrast to the violent, vitriolic, volatile succession of kings. The kings in the North botch their foreign relations and provoke the cruel Assyrians, who are probably the worst and most dangerous people we've seen in the whole Bible so far. Eventually, God judges Israel. Assyria carries the ten northern tribes away into captivity and the mists of history.

The Southern Kingdom of Judah Is Better: But still not great. In the South, Judah persists longer because of a few good kings who draw the people back toward God. Kings Hezekiah and Josiah get rid of idols and lead religious revivals. God blesses their reigns, but it's too little, too late.

The Fall of the South and the Temple Destroyed: After centuries of warning from prophets, God's judgment on His people for their rebellion and idolatry finally arrives in 586 BC in the form of Nebuchadnezzar of Babylon. The Babylonians conquer Jerusalem, deport her people, and completely obliterate Solomon's temple, where God dwelt among the people back at the beginning of this long chronicle of kings.

Hint of Hope: God had promised Adam, Abraham, and David that One would come who would redeem the mess, defeat the curse, and reign on David's throne forever, but as 1 and 2 Kings wraps up, things look bleak.

At the very end of the book, one last slave-king descended from David named Jehoiachin is released from jail while God's people are in exile, and he's invited to eat with the Babylonian king. It's not much, but it leaves us with the slightest bit of hope at the end of a brutal book.

Theme: The importance of covenant faithfulness to God, with faithful and faithless kings and the consequences of their actions as an example. Good kings submit to God; clown-kings think they're God.

Important Motifs: The royal line of King David, idolatry, faithfulness and faithlessness, miracles, fire from heaven, God's covenants with His people.

Key Verses: 1 Kings 9:1–9—This passage sums up 1 and 2 Kings and basically the plot of the whole Old Testament. Here's an abbreviated version, but it's worth looking it up and reading it all. The parts where God is talking are in italics:

> The LORD said to him [Solomon]:
>
> *"I have heard the prayer and plea you have made before me; I have consecrated this temple, which you have built, by putting my Name there forever. . . .*
>
> *"As for you, if you walk before me faithfully with integrity of heart and uprightness, as David your father did, and do all I command and observe my decrees and laws, I will establish your royal throne over Israel forever. . . .*

> *"But if you or your descendants turn away from me and do not observe the commands and decrees I have given you and go off to serve other gods and worship them, then I will cut off Israel from the land I have given them and will reject this temple I have consecrated for my Name."*

Most Quoted Moment: 1 Kings 18:21—"Elijah went before the people and said, 'How long will you waver between two opinions? If the Lord is God, follow him; but if Baal is God, follow him.'

"But the people said nothing."

Another Test Case: The book of Judges shows that anarchy can't break the curse of sin and death, and 1 and 2 Kings shows that human government can't break it either.

Most Shocking Moment: When Elijah gets taken up into heaven in a whirlwind. Or when Elisha summons bears to maul some jerk kids who were making fun of his male-pattern baldness (this is real; see 2 Kings 2:23–25).

Unsung Hero: Obadiah was the palace administrator for the dumpster-fire King Ahab and his bloodthirsty snake-wife Queen Jezebel.

Hezekiah's tunnel, a water tunnel, is found beneath the ancient city of David.

Артур Ильин/stock.adobe.com

When Jezebel orders all the faithful prophets of God to be killed, Obadiah risks his life by secretly hiding one hundred of them in a cave and providing them with food and water.

Most Controversial Part: In 1 Kings 11, the text says that Solomon had seven hundred wives, and they turned his heart after other gods.

Most Applicable Moment for Modern Audiences: Elijah feels beaten, exhausted, and alone in the face of evil, and then God speaks to him in a gentle whisper, reassuring him and telling him to get back in the fray.

If You Don't Have Time to Read the Whole Thing, at Least Read: The dedication of the temple from 1 Kings 8:1–9:9. Also, you'll love the prophet fight between Elijah and the prophets of Baal on Mount Carmel in 1 Kings 18:16–40. Finally, it's sad, but you should read about the fall of the North in 2 Kings 17 and the fall of the South in 2 Kings 25.

When You Visualize 1 and 2 Kings, Picture: A wicked king sacrificing to idols, and a good king holding up the law of God.

VITAL STATS

Position: 13 and 14 of 66.
Chapters: 65.
Verses: 1,764.
Word Count: 16,664 and 21,349 (18/66 and 9/66).
Most-Used Words: Son, David, father, descendants, Lord, king, God, Judah, Israel, temple, Solomon.
Group: Old Testament history.
Audience: Exiled Jews.
Date: 400ish BC.
Popularity Rank: 41 and 39 of 66.

1 & 2 CHRONICLES

Lightning-Fast Summary: An in-depth recap of the reigns of David and Solomon, along with quick coverage of all the kings of Judah who were descended from them.

Unique Feature: Chronicles, Kings, and Samuel combined make up roughly one-third of the entire narrative portions of the Bible.

Was This Originally One Big Book That Got Split in Two, Like What Happened to Samuel and Kings? Yes.

Years Covered: The book starts with a nine-chapter genealogy that goes all the way back to Adam, so if you count that, then Chronicles covers thousands of years. However, the action starts in chapter 10, and from there to the end of the book covers around five hundred years.

Who Wrote It? Anonymous, but whoever wrote it had a lot in common with Ezra the priest from the next two books of the Bible. So maybe Ezra, maybe not.

When It Was Written: The genealogy in 1 Chronicles 3 goes eight generations past Zerubbabel, who last appears in the 510s BC, so basic finger math says Chronicles must have been written a little after 400 BC in the later Persian Empire.

Original Language: Hebrew and then translated to Greek a couple hundred years later.

Original Audience: Jews who had their fortunes restored during the Persian Empire.

Type of Book: A largely positive theological history.

Tone and Feel: Dry for modern readers through the first nine chapters, but then juicy and even triumphalist for the rest of the book.

Why Do We Need This Book When We Already Have Kings? Kings was meant to make sense of God's judgment on Israel and Judah for the grieving exiles living in Babylon, so it focuses on the Jews' sin, idolatry, and failure. Chronicles, written one hundred fifty years later, is for a new moment in history. The Babylonians have been defeated, and their conquerors (the Persians) have allowed the return of the exiles and the rebuilding of the temple in Jerusalem. God has remembered and restored His people, and the book of Chronicles retells the story of the United Kingdom and then the Southern Kingdom of Judah with a positive framing to help the original audience understand *why* things are better and to help them know how to stay right with God as a people.

Samuel and Kings = Don't do this anymore.

Chronicles = Do more of this from now on.

Where It's Set: Mostly Judah, with an epilogue that takes us into Persia. Unlike Kings, Chronicles gives no attention to the lost Northern Kingdom of Israel, except for when their rulers come up briefly while telling the story of the Southern Kingdom.

Stuff You Can Still Physically Look At: There's an ancient carved monument called the Tel Dan Stele, which dates to the 700s or 800s BC, that names kings and places from Chronicles and specifically says "The House of David." It's in the Israel Museum in Jerusalem.

Parts You Might Recognize Even If You Haven't Read the Bible: Solomon building and dedicating the Jewish temple.

Important Characters: David, Solomon, Rehoboam, Hezekiah, and Josiah.

A Much Nicer History of the United Kingdom of Israel: Chronicles covers the death of Saul, the reign of David, and the reign of Solomon.

Chronicles assumes the reader is familiar with 1 and 2 Samuel and 1 and 2 Kings, and the Chronicler even alludes to those books as a source (as well as a ton of other now-lost books). With that in mind, Chronicles skips over the ugliest stuff from David's and Solomon's stories. There's no mention of David's affair with Bathsheba, nor of Solomon's hordes of wives and concubines or his idolatry later in life. Rather, Chronicles focuses on David's and Solomon's administrative prowess, military victories, wealth, and rock-solid reputation among other nations.

Lots of Good, a Little Bad, and Then a Hopeful Ending: The last half of 2 Chronicles takes us on a lightning-round tour of all the kings of Judah after Solomon up until Nebuchadnezzar and the Babylonians conquered Jerusalem and ended the kingdom in 586 BC. The Chronicler spends lots of time on the good kings and what they got right (especially Hezekiah and Josiah). The Chronicler also acknowledges all the bad kings, but usually only briefly mentions that they were disobedient to God before moving on to better things. The book ends, just like Kings, with an account of Babylon's conquest and the exile. However, unlike Kings, there's a little epilogue in the final two verses, where King Cyrus of Persia comes along and is moved by God to let the Jews go back to Jerusalem and rebuild the temple.

Theme: God keeps His promise to remember His people and restores them. Now Israel must learn from her past failures and be faithful to God.

Timeless Bonus Theme: God responds to repentance.

Important Motifs: The royal line of King David, idolatry, covenant, remembering, restoration.

Key Verse and Most Quoted Moment: 2 Chronicles 7:14 (God is talking to Solomon)—"If my people, who are called by my name, will humble themselves and pray and seek my face and turn from their wicked ways, then I will hear from heaven, and I will forgive their sin and will heal their land."

Most Shocking Moment: In 2 Chronicles 26, when King Uzziah struts into the temple to burn incense and God strikes him with leprosy, which made him ceremonially unclean for life.

Unsung Hero: Jehosheba, the fearless, quick-thinking wife of Jehoiada the stalwart priest. When the bloodthirsty Queen Athaliah became intent on snuffing out the royal line of David, Jehosheba hid Prince Joash in the temple for six years, after which Jehoiada put Joash in his rightful place on David's throne.

Most Applicable Moment for Modern Audiences: The restoration at the end is a reminder of God's forgiveness and remembrance even after failure and difficult consequences.

If You Don't Have Time to Read the Whole Thing, at Least Read: Solomon's blessing of the people at the dedication of the temple in 2 Chronicles 6, and then stick around to see God show up in the beginning of chapter 7.

When You Visualize 1 and 2 Chronicles, Picture: A recap montage featuring good kings.

VITAL STATS

Position: 15 of 66.
Chapters: 10.
Verses: 280.
Word Count: 5,605 (30/66).
Most-Used Words: God, king, Jerusalem, descendants, son, temple, Lord, house, Israel, men.
Group: Persian era history.
Audience: Jews who had returned to Judah from exile.
Date: After 430 BC.
Popularity Rank: 58 of 66.

EZRA

Lightning-Fast Summary: There's a new sheriff in town. Babylon is out; Persia is in. After living as exiles for fifty years, the Jews get to go back to Jerusalem to start the long process of rebuilding the temple and their people.

Unique Feature: Ezra and Nehemiah (the next book of the Bible) were treated as one book until the second century AD.

Who Wrote It? That's sort of the wrong question when we're talking about Ezra and Nehemiah. This book was more assembled than written. It tells a clean, cohesive story, but it does it with a bunch of components all lined up in order. Ezra consists of temple records, genealogies, lists of people who got things right, lists of people who blew it, regal decrees, letters, a long prayer, lyrics to a song, Ezra's memoirs, and a narrator's observations. Someone put it all together, but we don't know who.

Type of Book: Found-footage political thriller with stern prophetic undertones.

Tone and Feel: Laser-focused on meticulous accounting of what happened and what's expected moving forward.

Years Covered: About eighty years from 539 to 457 BC.

Parts You Might Recognize Even If You Haven't Read the Bible: The Persian Empire and her ultra-famous kings Cyrus, Darius, Xerxes, and Artaxerxes.

Stuff You Can Still Physically Look At: The Persian capitals of Susa and Persepolis.

Original Language: Hebrew, but also a lot of Aramaic. The Persians did international business in Aramaic, so all but one of the official letters in Ezra are in Aramaic.

Important Characters: The Persian kings, Jeshua, Zerubbabel, Tattenai, and Ezra.

Know Before Reading: This book assumes you already know the following:

- God picked Abraham and his descendants as His chosen people.
- Abraham's descendants worshiped idols and disobeyed God for centuries.
- In a five-hundred-year-long slow-motion tragedy, the Israelite kingdom split, turned evil, and was destroyed.
- The killing blow was struck by Nebuchadnezzar of Babylon, who destroyed the temple in Jerusalem and took the Jewish people into exile about fifty years before the beginning of the book of Ezra.
- God promised to restore His people if they ever changed their ways and returned to following Him.

Very Important History Stuff: Babylon conquered Jerusalem and destroyed the temple in 586 BC. In 539 BC, Persia's Cyrus the Great conquered Babylon and turned out to be way more powerful but also way nicer than the Babylonians. Within a year of taking over, Cyrus gave the Jews back all the temple treasures that Nebuchadnezzar had stolen and told them to go back and rebuild the temple in Jerusalem.

Ezra Is a Book About Two Quests: First, rebuild the temple. Second, rebuild the people.

Quest Number One (Ezra 1–6): Zerubbabel (a descendant of David who would have been king if there was still a kingdom) leads the quest to return and rebuild the temple in Jerusalem. It starts well, but the project bogs down in the face of apathy and obnoxious opposition from all sides. Cyrus dies, and his successors defy his decree to allow the Jews to rebuild the temple. Finally, twenty years later, after a dramatic rediscovery of Cyrus's lost order, and with the insistent prodding of the prophets Haggai and Zechariah, the Jews complete the temple and dedicate it in 516 BC—seventy years after the last one was destroyed.

What's Going On with the Timeline? Ezra takes a leap forward in time in Ezra 4 to show that the Jews face resistance in their quests from the time of Cyrus all the way up to the time he writes the book. This historical aside makes sense when you're looking for it, but it can be confusing on your first pass.

About fifty years pass between the end of Ezra 6 and the beginning of Ezra 7. The entire story of the book of Esther happens between these two chapters during that fifty-year gap.

Quest Number Two (Ezra 7–10): After the temple had been up and running for fifty years (and all the sacrifices, festivals, and rituals that go along with that), the new king of Persia, Artaxerxes, sent Ezra the priest to Jerusalem. Ezra's quest was to teach the Jews the law of God and to effectively rebuild the people. In Jerusalem, Ezra discovers that the Jews are marrying their pagan neighbors and starting back down the path to idolatry that brought the judgment of God on them and landed them in exile in the first place. The offenders apologize and divorce their foreign wives en masse.

One Down, One to Go: The book of Ezra ends with the temple quest completed but the quest of rebuilding the people still unfinished. Quest number two carries over into the book of Nehemiah.

Theme: God keeps His promise to remember His people and reverses their fortunes. In doing so, He solidifies His plan to redeem fallen humanity.

Important Motifs: A people set apart, intermarriage, repentance, God directing the hearts of kings, remembrance, God's covenants with His people.

Key Verse: Ezra 1:3 (part of the decree of Cyrus)—"Any of his people among you may go up to Jerusalem in Judah and build the temple of the Lord, the God of Israel, the God who is in Jerusalem, and may their God be with them."

Also Read: Nehemiah, Esther, Haggai, Zechariah.

Why Ezra (and Nehemiah) Matter to the Story: It shows God's character in keeping His promises, but it also represents one last try on the part of the Jews to finally get everything perfectly right before the Old Testament ends.

Most Shocking Moment: Out of the blue, Cyrus lets the Jews go home. It can't be overstated how stunning a reversal of fortune this is in the flow of the Old Testament story.

Most Controversial Part: Ezra makes everyone divorce their foreign wives.

Unsung Hero: Shekaniah son of Jehiel, who swallows his pride and supports Ezra by admitting in front of the people that they should not have intermarried with their pagan neighbors.

Most Applicable Moment for Modern Audiences: The collective repentance of Ezra and the people.

If You Don't Have Time to Read the Whole Thing, at Least Read: The second half of Ezra 3, where the foundation of the temple is dedicated. The young people cheer, but the old-timers, who remember the size and splendor of Solomon's temple, weep.

When You Visualize Ezra, Picture: A shiny new temple, standing in the rubble of the old one.

VITAL STATS

Position: 16 of 66.
Chapters: 13.
Verses: 406.
Word Count: 8,507 (27/66).
Most-Used Words: Son, God, people, Levites, Jerusalem, men.
Group: Persian era history.
Audience: Jews who had returned to Judah from exile.
Date: After 430 BC.
Popularity Rank: 44 of 66.

NEHEMIAH

Lightning-Fast Summary: Nehemiah, the Jewish cupbearer to the king of Persia, finds out Jerusalem is in peril. With the king's blessing, he rebuilds the walls and fortifies the Jewish people.

Unique Feature: Nehemiah is the rest of Ezra. In the book of Ezra, the main characters have two quests. The first is to rebuild the temple (that one is completed in Ezra), and the second is to rebuild the people after ages of bad stuff. Ezra the priest makes progress on the second quest, but restoring the Jewish people and securing their future in Jerusalem is still the mission in view as we turn the page from Ezra to Nehemiah.

Who Wrote It? We don't know who put it all together, but it contains some of Nehemiah's very personal memoirs.

Type of Book: Found-footage political thriller from the perspective of a no-nonsense leader who just wants to get the job done.

Tone and Feel: It's a lot like Ezra, but we get to know Nehemiah better, and he comes off as honest and reflective. This gives the book of Nehemiah a little more humanity than the book of Ezra.

Amount of Time Covered: About a year, probably in 444 BC.

Parts You Might Recognize Even If You Haven't Read the Bible: King Artaxerxes of Persia.

Stuff You Can Still Physically Look At: One little section of the wall Nehemiah built in Jerusalem.

Original Language: Hebrew, with some Aramaic, which makes sense because Aramaic was an official language of the Persian Empire.

Important Characters: Nehemiah, Ezra, Artaxerxes, Sanballat, Tobiah, Geshem, Eliashib.

Very Important History Stuff: The Southern Kingdom of Judah fell to the Babylonians in 586 BC. They destroyed the temple and made the Jews exiles in Babylon. Fifty years later, the Persians conquered Babylon and let the Jews go back to Jerusalem to rebuild the temple, starting in 538 BC. They completed and dedicated the temple in 516 BC, seventy years after the first temple was destroyed, as predicted by the prophet Jeremiah. All this is covered in Ezra 1–6. Things turned sour in the 470s, when a Persian official named Haman nearly succeeded in wiping out all the Jews before his plan was thwarted by Persian King Xerxes's secretly Jewish wife, Esther. Xerxes was assassinated in 465 BC, and his son Artaxerxes emerged as the new king. At the outset of Nehemiah, old enemies of the Jews, who also live under Persian rule, are rattling the saber against Jerusalem and the temple.

Nehemiah Takes Up the Quest: Nehemiah is the loyal cupbearer and friend to the king. Artaxerxes generously allows Nehemiah to travel, with authority, to Jerusalem to fend off the wolves and rebuild her dilapidated walls. Nehemiah is presented as a man who knows the story of his people and who knows exactly where he fits in the unfolding of that story. With the king's blessing, he snaps into action. He powers past critics, red tape, and saboteurs, and with a sword in one hand and a trowel in the other, he leads the ragtag citizens of Jerusalem to complete the new city walls in just fifty-two days.

The enemies outside the walls skulk away defeated, but Nehemiah uncovers corruption among the people of Jerusalem. With the help of Ezra the priest, he roots it out. Protected by the freshly completed walls, Ezra and Nehemiah set up a public reading of the Book of the Law of God in Jerusalem. They pause as they read to explain everything in normal human language to the people to make sure the Jews truly get who God is and what His laws are about. Then the people confess their sins as a group and publicly recommit themselves to the ancient covenant with God.

The book ends with both quests of Ezra and Nehemiah completed.

And They All Lived Happily Ever After: Well, sadly, no. Even in the final paragraphs of Nehemiah, the attentive reader can tell that his reforms may unravel as soon as Nehemiah and Ezra aren't there to hold it all together. Even Nehemiah seems exhausted at the end of the book as he recounts his efforts to get it all straightened out.

A hundred years later, Persia fell to Alexander the Great, and a little more than 150 years after that (in 167 BC), the Jewish people won their independence. But after a century of corrupt leaders and internal strife, that Jewish kingdom ended at the hands of the Romans.

What Ezra and Nehemiah Accomplished: The reforms of Ezra and Nehemiah brought about religious renewal, strengthened Jewish identity, and positioned the Jews to endure the fall of Persia and the Greek cultural tidal wave set in motion by Alexander the Great.

What Ezra and Nehemiah *Didn't* Accomplish: They didn't solve the human problem. Even with the support of the Persian Empire and all her resources, even with a huge religious revival, even with a rebuilt temple, and even with the ancestral city of Jerusalem fully fortified against her enemies, the people still couldn't hold up their end of the covenant with God.

Even after the best try that God's chosen people put forth in the whole Old Testament, it was still clear that God would have to do all the heavy lifting to defeat sin, death, and the curse.

Theme: *Remembrance*. Nehemiah uses this word a lot as a request for God to punish His enemies and as a request for God's mercy on the faithful. The book ends with Nehemiah saying, "Remember me with favor, my God" (13:31).

The Broad Wall is an ancient defensive wall in the old city of Jerusalem. It dates to the late eighth century BC during the reign of King Hezekiah.

Important Motifs: Courage, a people set apart, intermarriage, repentance, God directing the hearts of kings, covenant.

Key Verses: Nehemiah 1:4–11, particularly in verses 8 and 9 when Nehemiah reminds God of His promise to restore His people from long ago—"Remember the instruction you gave your servant Moses, saying, 'If you are unfaithful, I will scatter you among the nations, but if you return to me and obey my commands, then even if your exiled people are at the farthest horizon, I will gather them from there and bring them to the place I have chosen as a dwelling for my Name.'"

Also Read: Ezra, Esther.

Most Shocking Moment: Nehemiah finds out the priest Eliashib was selling out his own people to the enemies of the Jews.

Most Controversial Part: Just as in Ezra, Nehemiah oversees another mass divorce from the neighboring pagans.

Funniest Part: Nehemiah's enemies claim he's preparing a rebellion against Artaxerxes. Nehemiah says in 6:8, "Nothing like what you are saying is happening; you are just making it up out of your head." And then he goes right back to work on the wall.

Unsung Hero: Hanani, who travels a thousand miles each way just to tell Nehemiah about the state of things in Jerusalem.

Most Applicable Moment for Modern Audiences: Nehemiah's knowledge of the big story of God and where he fits into it positions him to act with clear-minded, principled courage in the face of long odds and resistance.

If You Don't Have Time to Read the Whole Thing, at Least Read: Nehemiah 1 and 13.

When You Visualize Nehemiah, Picture: That wall.

VITAL STATS

Position: 17 of 66.

Chapters: 10.

Verses: 167.

Word Count: 4,932 (32/66).

Most-Used Words: King, queen, Jews, nobles, royal, month.

Group: Persian era history.

Audience: Jews all over the Persian Empire.

Date: Between 465 BC and 331 BC.

Popularity Rank: 47 of 66.

Lightning-Fast Summary: The king of Persia has a contest to pick a new queen and chooses a secret Jew named Esther. The king's right-hand man hates Jews and hatches a plan to kill them all, but Esther finds out and turns the tables on him, saving her people. The Jews commemorate this by creating a new annual festival called Purim.

Unique Feature: Esther is the only book of the Bible that definitively does not mention God.

Strong Female Lead: Esther is a three-dimensional character with struggles and flaws. She matures as the story goes along and boldly comes through in the end.

Who Wrote It? It's anonymous. Whoever it was knows a lot about Persian culture and the inner working of the palace at Susa but is also enthusiastically Jewish.

Type of Book: High-stakes historical drama that literally has high stakes (the bad guys get impaled at the end of the story).

Tone and Feel: This book knows it's great and delights in telling the juicy story of a grand reversal of fortune in a way that's vividly colorful and unapologetically pro-Jewish.

When It Was Written: After the reign of King Xerxes of Persia, who was assassinated in 465 BC, and before the arrival of Alexander the Great in 331 BC. Ancient accounts suggest that Esther was the last book of the Old Testament to be written.

Original Audience: Jews scattered around the Persian Empire.

Time Covered: About ten years, starting in 483 BC.

Parts You Might Recognize Even If You Haven't Read the Bible: Xerxes scored a famous victory at the Battle of Thermopylae over King Leonidas and his three hundred Spartans before being defeated and run out of Greece by the Athenians and their allies.

Stuff You Can Still Physically Look At: The ruins of the palace in Susa, where this whole political thriller played out. You can also still see Jews around the world celebrating Purim to this day.

Original Language: Hebrew, with a few loan words from Old Persian.

Important Characters: Xerxes, Esther, Mordecai, Haman, Vashti.

Where Esther Fits in the Larger Bible: The entire story of Esther happens between the end of Ezra 6 and the beginning of Ezra 7.

Esther, the Secret Jewish Queen of Persia: The book opens with Xerxes planning his ill-fated invasion of Greece. When his wife, Vashti, refuses to "entertain" Xerxes and his noble buddies, the king deposes her. Time passes, and Xerxes is sad (probably because he lost to the Greeks), so he hosts a contest to find a new wife. A Jewish orphan named Esther becomes the darling of the contest and wins the king's hand, but she hides her ethnicity. When her uncle, Mordecai, discovers a plot against Xerxes, Esther proves her courage and loyalty by relaying the details to the king, saving his life.

A Plot to Kill All the Jews: Xerxes's go-to man Haman was descended from an ancient enemy of the Jews, so when Mordecai doesn't bow to him in the streets of Susa, Haman convinces Xerxes to order all the Jews in the empire to be killed and decides to have Mordecai impaled. Haman chooses the date of the massacre by rolling something like ancient dice called *pur*.

Esther Saves the Jews: Esther finds out about the plot and weaves a clever plan to expose Haman while making sure not to embarrass her husband. She reveals her secret Jewish identity, Haman wilts, and Xerxes has Haman impaled on the gallows he built for Mordecai. Esther and Mordecai help the king craft a counterorder that allows all the Jews to fight back on the appointed day, and the Jews completely destroy those who had been sharpening their knives in anticipation. When it's all over, Mordecai sends out letters to the Jews empire-wide, telling them to remember how their people were saved by celebrating a new annual festival named for the dice rolled by the wicked Haman: *Purim*.

Save the Jews, Save the World: An entire people getting saved from annihilation is a story worth telling, but Esther is more than a story of human triumph. Throughout the whole Old Testament, from Abraham to Moses to David, God has hitched His plan to break the curse and redeem humanity to the Jewish people. He promises that the serpent-crushing, curse-lifting, eternal-throne-sitting Savior of everything is going to come through them. If Haman would've had his way, God's redemptive plan would have been extinguished, along with the Jewish people. But instead Haman lost, God won, and the redemptive plan is still on.

Theme: *Providence*. God doesn't even have to be mentioned in this book to be seen as Master over the unfolding of events. What seems like luck, fortune, or fate at first is actually the providence of God to accomplish His purposes.

The Clown-King Motif: Kings throughout the Bible are often portrayed as fools who imagine themselves to be God and answer to no one. Xerxes, like many other Bible kings, looks absurd in his blustering and self-contradiction when contrasted with God, the one true King, who is the most powerful character in a story, even when His name goes unmentioned.

Most Quoted Verse: Mordecai persuades Esther to muster her courage and speak to Xerxes, even though he hasn't summoned her (which was illegal under penalty of death). She balks at first, but then steels herself and famously says, "I will go to the king, even though it is against the law. And if I perish, I perish" (4:16).

Theme Verse: While he's making his case to Esther, Mordecai gets the most important theological line in the whole book when he says, "For if you remain silent at this time, relief and deliverance for the Jews will arise from another place, but you and your father's family will perish. And who knows but that you have come to your royal position for such a time as this?" (Esther 4:14).

Mordecai seems to know that God, though unmentioned, is fully in command of the situation, and one way or another, He will work events to deliver His people, no matter what Esther or anyone chooses.

Also Read: Ezra, Nehemiah.

Most Shocking Moment: Haman gets impaled on the stake (or hung on the gallows, depending on the translation) he built for Mordecai.

Most Controversial Part: Esther asks Xerxes for one additional day for the Jews to destroy their enemies in Susa, and the king says yes.

Unsung Heroes: Hegai, Hathak, and Harbona—three Persian eunuchs who discreetly had Esther's back at pivotal moments.

Most Applicable Moment for Modern Audiences: Esther equivocating at first but then finding the courage to do the right thing.

If You Don't Have Time to Read the Whole Thing, at Least Read: If you start this book, you won't put it down. Just read the whole thing.

When You Visualize Esther, Picture: The pur. Haman thinks he and fate are in the driver's seat, but God is in charge all along.

Ruins of the palace of Darius in Susa.

Carole Raddato/CC BY-SA 2.0

VITAL STATS

Position: 18 of 66.
Chapters: 42.
Verses: 1,070.
Word Count: 12,674 (22/66).
Most-Used Words: God, man, does, Job, words, earth, eyes, Almighty.
Group: Wisdom Literature.
Audience: Followers of God and anyone who thinks about the big questions of life, death, and God.
Date: Unsure, but very old.
Popularity Rank: 23 of 66.

Lightning-Fast Summary: God allows a righteous man named Job to suffer severely at the hands of Satan. Job and his friends try to make sense of his suffering, but in the end, God Himself shows up to speak to it, and everyone is left silent in the face of His glory, power, and rightness.

Unique Feature: The book of Job tells a story, but it doesn't present itself in the same historical manner as the previous seventeen books of the Bible. It mentions a setting (the unknown land of Uz), but there are no rulers or reigns by which to assign it a date. The timeless theme of trying to understand suffering comes through more clearly because of this.

50 percent: The end of Job marks the halfway point of the Bible.

Who Wrote It? We don't know.

Type of Book: Job is the first book in the Wisdom Literature section of the Bible; it uses glimpses into the heavenly throne room of God, long philosophical conversations among friends, and a tour of creation hosted by God Himself to process through human suffering and God's character.

Tone and Feel: Deeply reflective, earnest, thorough in processing some of the biggest questions in life.

When It Was Written: There are hints that the story might be set and initially recorded in very ancient times, even thousands of years before Jesus, but subtle details in the text hint that the book, as it comes to us, was written sometime after 1000 BC. No other book in the Bible has so much mystery surrounding its origins.

Original Audience: Followers of God who experienced meaningful suffering and were trying to make sense of it.

Time Covered: Unclear, but probably several months.

Job, the Renaissance Man: Job is presented as a well-rounded, scholarly man. He knew plenty about celestial motion, mining, biology, botany, economics, ethics, philosophy, rhetoric, and more. And he saw meaning in all of that.

Parts You Might Recognize Even If You Haven't Read the Bible: Stories about the suffering of Job.

Stuff You Can Still Physically Look At: Nothing. Job isn't set clearly in history like all the books that precede it in the Bible.

Original Language: Hebrew.

Important Characters: God, Satan, Job, Eliphaz, Bildad, Zophar, Elihu.

A Strange Meeting: In the first two chapters of Job, Satan suggests to God that His faithful servant Job is only faithful because God protects him from suffering. God allows Satan to inflict all kinds of terrible suffering on Job, but Job still won't curse God.

A Frustrating Conversation with "Friends": For the next thirty-five chapters, Job and four friends try to work through what happened. Eliphaz, Bildad, and Zophar all believe in God but don't do a great job of consoling Job. They all think suffering only happens as a result of sin, so they accuse Job of secret sin and tell him to repent in order to be spared further pain and to receive blessings from God again. Job defends himself. He thinks sin alone isn't an explanation for all his suffering, and the conversation spirals until Job sounds bitter and his friends sound cruel in the face of his pain. Elihu, a fourth friend, eventually chimes in. He rejects the simplistic karmic thinking of Eliphaz, Bildad, and Zophar and accuses Job of imagining himself to be God's equal in wisdom and judgment. Elihu points to the goodness, power, and majesty of God and intones that the other four men are coming at the question of suffering pridefully and wrongheadedly.

Then God Shows Up to Settle Things: While in the throes of suffering, many have wished God would show up and explain Himself, and in Job, that actually happens. But it doesn't go how Job probably imagined it would. God opens the conversation by asking, "Who is this that obscures my plans with words without knowledge? Brace yourself like a man; I will question *you,* and you shall answer me" (38:2–3, italics added).

For the next four chapters, God takes Job on a whirlwind tour of existence to illustrate Job's tininess and God's infinite power and knowledge. After humbling Job to nothing, God asks, "Would you discredit my justice? Would you condemn me to justify yourself?" (Job 40:8).

Job repents of his pride. God tells Eliphaz, Bildad, and Zophar that they were wrong and that in the end Job was right. Finally, God blesses Job for the rest of his very long life in terms that an ancient audience would understand to be lavishly generous on God's part.

The Point: In the end, Job and friends never came close to guessing what was actually going on and why Job had suffered. But Elihu was right in saying God's ways are higher and that His character is good. God is attentive to Job's suffering but makes it clear to Job that the only right response to God's power and glory is submission and faith.

Theme: Suffering is real, and God cares about it (that's why He's in the process of redeeming all things, which is what the story of the Bible is). Also, we aren't well-positioned to understand suffering, but God is, and He's good. In light of that, our only play is to trust God and submit to Him.

Did the Stuff in Job Actually Happen? Maybe. Job is ancient wisdom literature. It's a different genre than the historical books of the Bible, and it's unclear whether these events are to be understood as having literally occurred or whether this is a story crafted to wrestle through crucial questions. Either way, Christians believe it's inspired by God, and it accomplishes exactly what God wants it to accomplish.

Theme Verse: Job's initial response to his suffering in Job 1:21—"The Lord gave and the Lord has taken away; may the name of the Lord be praised." Job understandably struggled in this conviction, but at the end of the book, he ends up back where he started—trusting God.

Also Read: Ecclesiastes. Job is about what happens when everything goes wrong, but Ecclesiastes talks a lot about what happens when everything goes right.

Most Shocking Moment: When God, who's apparently been listening to the whole conversation, shows up and gives the final word on everything.

Most Controversial Part: When God lets Satan harm His servant Job. Obviously.

Unsung Hero: Elihu, who keeps his mouth shut for thirty-plus chapters and then comes in and basically says what God goes on to say. Of the five main conversationalists, he's the only one God doesn't correct.

What Would Happen If Job Weren't in the Bible? The Bible would seem out of step with reality for never deeply exploring the problem of pain and suffering.

Most Applicable Moment for Modern Audiences: Job realizing the vastness of God and being humbled.

If You Don't Have Time to Read the Whole Thing, at Least Read: All of Job 38 so you can hear God speak to suffering in His own words.

When You Visualize Job, Picture: Job covered in boils and ashes.

VITAL STATS

Position: 19 of 66.
Chapters: 150.
Verses: 2,461.
Word Count: 30,147 (3/66).
Most-Used Words: Lord, God, praise, heart, love, sing, righteous, enemies, people, salvation.
Group: The Psalms (Wisdom Literature).
Audience: Jews in the age of Babylon and Persia.
Date: Completed in the 400s BC.
Popularity Rank: 1 of 66.

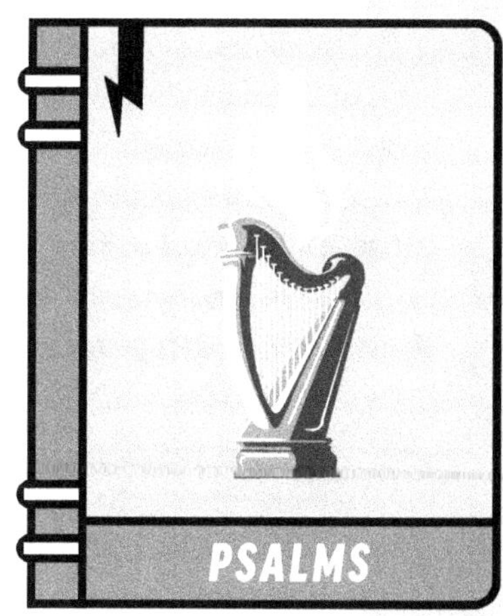

PSALMS

Lightning-Fast Summary: A collection of the best poems, prayers, and songs about God from the ancient Israelite people.

Unique Feature: Psalms might simultaneously be the oldest book of the Old Testament and the youngest. Psalm 90 was written by Moses before the five books of the Law were completed in the 1400s BC. Psalms 126 and 137 were likely written in the Persian era during the rebuilding of Jerusalem in the 400s BC. Not many books take a thousand years to write.

Who Wrote It? David, Asaph, the sons of Korah, Solomon, Moses, Heman, and Ethan.

Type of Book: An anthology of poems, prayers, and songs assembled from across the centuries by unknown anthologists.

Tone and Feel: Just like the songs you listen to, it depends. Some are thankful, others repentant, still others angry.

How It's Built: Psalms contains five books. Book one is Psalms 1–41, book two is Psalms 42–72, book three is 73–89, book four is 90–106, and book five is 107–150. These books are organized by themes and purpose more than by the order in which they were written.

When It Was Finished: The final round of psalms and the five-book structure were probably finished in the 400s BC.

Original Audience: The final form was assembled for devout Jews living after the Babylonian exile in the late 500s to the 400s BC.

Parts You Might Recognize Even If You Haven't Read the Bible: The twenty-third psalm, which starts, "The Lord is my shepherd, I lack nothing. He makes me lie down in green pastures . . ." (vv. 1–2). It's one of the three most famous passages in the whole Bible. It's familiar to many, even those who aren't Christians.

Original Language: Hebrew with a tiny bit of Aramaic (as in Psalm 2:12).

Important Characters: God is overtly the central and most-mentioned character in Psalms.

Historical Setting: It's possible to figure out when and where across the history of the Old Testament lots of the psalms were written. They hit harder when you know what was going on when they were composed. One example is Psalm 51. It's a prayerful song of repentance that David wrote after he had an affair with Bathsheba and then had her husband killed. In verse 17, he writes, "My sacrifice, O God, is a broken spirit; a broken and contrite heart you, God, will not despise."

Theme: Psalms contains heartfelt responses to God from across the spectrum of human experience. The themes of gratitude and submission to God in all circumstances permeate the whole book.

Theme Verse: Psalm 46:1—"God is our refuge and strength, an ever-present help in trouble."

Finished All 150 and Still Want More Psalms? Check out these bonus psalms from around the Bible:

- the song of Moses and Miriam in Exodus 15
- the song of Moses in Deuteronomy 32
- the song of Deborah in Judges 5
- Hannah's prayer in 1 Samuel 2
- the song of the vineyard in Isaiah 5
- the song of Hezekiah in Isaiah 38

- King David's song of thanksgiving in 2 Samuel 22
- Mary's song (also called *the Magnificat*) in Luke 1
- the song of Zechariah (also called *the Benedictus*) in Luke 1
- the songs of the Suffering Servant in Isaiah 42, 49, 50, and 52–53

Some of These Songs Seem Very Angry: Yes, fancy Bible people call these imprecatory psalms. They're emotionally charged requests for God's judgment against enemies and God's justice for the psalmist. In Psalm 69, David pleads, "Save me, O God, for the waters have come up to my neck," and "Pour out your wrath on them; let your fierce anger overtake them" (vv. 1, 24). Other examples include Psalms 5, 10, and 109. Go check them out, but be advised: They're spicy.

Why the Psalms Are in the Bible: The people in the Bible were like us. They had amazing moments, nightmare disasters, and everything in between, and they wrote songs, poems, and prayers in response that say true things about their walk with God and about God Himself. Psalms artistically gives us the gritty, painful, euphoric truth of things in the raw language of emotion but with the precision crafting of timeless art.

If You Don't Have Time to Read the Whole Thing, at Least Read: Psalms 1 and 2, which frame up the whole collection; Psalm 23; Psalm 22, uttered by Jesus while He was dying on the cross; and Psalm 110, which is the most-quoted psalm in the New Testament.

When You Visualize Psalms, Picture: A handheld harp.

VITAL STATS

Position: 20 of 66.
Chapters: 31.
Verses: 915.
Word Count: 9,921 (24/66).
Most-Used Words: Wisdom, knowledge, understanding, righteous, fool, instruction, fear.
Group: Wisdom Literature.
Audience: Israel.
Date: Finished by the early 600s BC.
Popularity Rank: 7 of 66.

PROVERBS

Lightning-Fast Summary: A collection of wise sayings for living rightly before God.

Unique Feature: Proverbs is the most unapologetically practical book in the Bible. It has some structure to it, but at the most basic level, it's a stack of the best moral-ethical-commonsensical teachings from Old Testament times.

How to Understand the Proverbs: They aren't promises from God, laws, or prophecies; rather, the proverbs are witty, memorable truisms born out of the values of God that speak to wise, upright living on a wide variety of topics.

They Always at Least Describe What Generally Happens: Some proverbs describe a universal truth (9:10—"The fear of the LORD is the beginning of wisdom"). Many others convey wisdom by describing how things generally go, even though exceptions may exist (22:6—"Start children off on the way they should go, and even when they are old they will not turn from it").

Who Wrote It? Solomon, Agur, King Lemuel, and possibly more (but mostly Solomon).

When It Was Written: Solomon ruled in the 900s BC, so any proverb he wrote dates to that time period, but it looks like Solomon was drawing on previous wisdom as well, meaning parts of Proverbs might be much older. We don't know when the other authors of Proverbs wrote.

When Did Proverbs Reach Its Final Form? Mostly or entirely during the reign of Hezekiah from 715–686 BC.

What Qualifies Solomon to Give Advice? In 1 Kings 3, God appears to Solomon and tells the king that He'll grant him whatever he asks for. Solomon asks for "a discerning heart to govern your people and to distinguish between right and wrong" (v. 9). God is pleased with the answer and says, "I will give you a wise and discerning heart, so that there will never have been anyone like you, nor will there ever be" (v. 12). Even though Solomon ignored his own discernment at times, especially later in his reign, he is still held out as being remarkable in his wisdom and judgment.

Tone and Feel: Pleasantly instructive, like the voice of someone who accumulated a ton of expensive, hard-earned lessons and now wants to pass them on to others at a more affordable cost to them.

How It's Built:

- Part 1. The first third of the book contains proverbs written (or at least collected and organized) by Solomon, who is using them to instruct his sons. The teaching is timeless, but sadly, we learn from other parts of the Bible that Solomon's sons didn't fully internalize these nine chapters.
- Part 2. From chapter 10 to chapter 24, we get the main body of the book, which is a rapid-fire series of Solomon's favorite proverbs on a ton of different subjects, along with a few other "Sayings of the Wise."
- Part 3. Around 700 BC, good king Hezekiah compiled a bunch of Solomon's proverbs, which are listed in chapters 25 through 29.
- Part 4. Chapter 30 has the proverbs of Agur. We don't know anything about him, but he was clearly a wise man.
- Part 5. Chapter 31 starts with a few sayings from the otherwise unknown King Lemuel.
- Part 6. The rest of chapter 31 describes the characteristics of a wife of noble character.

Original Audience: Some of it was originally written to Solomon's sons, but all of it was for the people of Israel, probably the young people of Israel, in particular.

Phrases from Proverbs You Might Recognize Even If You Haven't Read the Bible:

- "Pride goes before destruction." (16:18)
- "As iron sharpens iron, so one person sharpens another." (27:17)
- "A gentle answer turns away wrath." (15:1)

Original Language: Hebrew.

Important Characters: Solomon, his son, Lady Wisdom, the woman of noble character.

Theme Verse and Theme: Proverbs 9:10—"The fear of the LORD is the beginning of wisdom." Proverbs is about wisdom rightly applied.

Who Is Lady Wisdom? She's the personification of wisdom in the form of a thoughtful, refined, noble woman of influence. She appears from time to time in early Proverbs to beckon readers toward righteousness and understanding.

Why Is Proverbs in the Bible? First and foremost, it's to help people, using very straightforward, understandable, practical language. Wisdom is better than folly, and walking on the road of righteousness and understanding is better than walking down the path of foolishness.

If You Like Proverbs, Definitely Also Read: Job and Ecclesiastes. Those two books deal with the outliers (extreme suffering and extreme comfort) and exceptions to the proverbs.

If You Don't Have Time to Read the Whole Thing, at Least Read: Proverbs 1:7, and then pick any random twenty-five proverbs from Proverbs 10–29 and see what you get.

When You Visualize Proverbs, Picture: Lady Wisdom.

VITAL STATS

Position: 21 of 66.
Chapters: 12.
Verses: 222.
Word Count: 4,537 (34/66).
Most-Used Words: Vanity, wisdom, toil, under the sun, man, God, time, meaningless.
Group: Wisdom Literature.
Audience: The Israelites and anyone who wonders about life.
Date: Hard to say.
Popularity Rank: 29 of 66.

ECCLESIASTES

Happy Lightning-Fast Summary: A wise and successful man invites the reader to reflect with him on the meaning of life.

Bleaker (but Still Fair) Lightning-Fast Summary: Life feels meaningless, and we're all going to die soon.

Unique Feature: The Hebrew word *hevel*. You'll see it translated as "vanity," "meaningless," or "breath." It's hard to capture the exact meaning of the concept in English, and that's ironic/appropriate, because *hevel* means just that—something that's hard to hold on to, something you can't lock down and keep. The idea that everything is fleeting is the central idea of the book.

Sounds Sad—Is It? Yes, and no. The tone of Ecclesiastes, like the idea of *hevel*, is hard to pin down. The author seems distraught that everything in life slips through one's fingers, and that time eventually devours everything, but these somber realizations force the author to think through how best to live. Ecclesiastes is a brutal reality check paired with a sensible response to the situation we all find ourselves in as mortals.

Who Wrote It? The host of the book calls himself only "the Teacher," but we find out he's insanely rich, king in

Jerusalem, son of David, and obviously exceptionally wise, so there's a good chance "the Teacher" is Solomon.

When It Was Written: After the reign of David and before Alexander the Great (330s BC). If Solomon is the author, then it was written in the 900s BC in Jerusalem.

Why This Title? Ecclesiastes is a Latin translation of a Hebrew word for someone who leads an assembly (the Teacher).

Tone and Feel: Restless, honest, seeking.

An Amazing Trifecta of Books About Life: Proverbs provides wisdom in light of how things normally go in life. Job has wisdom for exceptional suffering. Ecclesiastes tackles the numbness and melancholy we feel when everything is good. These three books cover the whole gamut of human circumstances.

Poolside Reflections from Someone Who Has It All: Right after he lets us know he's a king, the Teacher throws down the gauntlet, saying everything is *hevel* (meaningless, vapor, vanity). Work, pleasure, achievement, money, wisdom (even folly)—all vanity, all meaningless. Chapters 3–4 read like the reflections of an old billionaire in a bathrobe sitting by his empty pool, swirling his drink, and monologuing about how the world works. It's sobering to hear someone who has had unimaginable success admit that there's no pot of clarity and meaning at the end of the rainbow if you just have enough money, fame, and power.

Eventually, the Teacher circles back around to wisdom and recites a few of his favorite proverbs before acknowledging that things don't always go according to the way the proverbs say. Finally, he concludes that wisdom is still better than folly, that life is short so people should enjoy the work God has given them in the here and now, and that since we can't ultimately solve the enigma of *hevel*, our best bet is to obey God and trust Him.

Original Audience: It's originally for the people of Israel, but the themes are so universal that it may as well have been written for anyone at any time.

Phrases from Ecclesiastes You Might Recognize Even If You Haven't Read the Bible:

- "To every thing there is a season, and a time to every purpose under the heaven." (3:1 KJV)
- "A time to be born, and a time to die; a time to plant, and a time to pluck up that which is planted." (3:2 KJV)
- "There is nothing new under the sun." (1:9)
- "The race is not to the swift or the battle to the strong." (9:11)

Original Language: Hebrew.

Theme Verse: Ecclesiastes 1:2—"'Meaningless! Meaningless!' says the Teacher. 'Utterly meaningless! Everything is meaningless.'"

Relevant Bonus Verse from Somewhere Else: Psalm 90:12—"Teach us to number our days, that we may gain a heart of wisdom."

This Book Requires Courage: Ecclesiastes asks you to stare down some very hard stuff. The Teacher feels like no matter how much he tightens his grip, all the beautiful things in his life still slip through his fingers eventually. This is true for everyone, whether we like to think about it or not.

The Teacher is dead honest about the human problem and makes it clear that if *he* can't solve it with all he has, then *you* can't solve it either.

The Teacher shares his best take on what to do about the meaninglessness of life in the final chapter, and it's at least something.

Remember the Curse from Genesis? That's the human problem. That's what Ecclesiastes is about. That's what the Teacher can't outwit. That's what plagues you and me. We're getting toward the end of the Old Testament. We've tried everything, and the curse of sin and death and toil is still there.

Keep Reading—It Gets Better: Jesus, the centerpiece of God's redemptive plan, is going to show up after a few more books and defeat the curse. If Ecclesiastes hits a little too close to home, you're going to love the Jesus stuff.

If You Don't Have Time to Read the Whole Thing, at Least Read: Ecclesiastes 1 for the theme of time, then Ecclesiastes 11 for the theme of mortality, and Ecclesiastes 12 for the resolution.

When You Visualize Ecclesiastes, Picture: Vapor solidifying in the hands of God.

VITAL STATS

Position: 22 of 66.
Chapters: 8.
Verses: 117.
Word Count: 2,020 (44/66).
Most-Used Words: Beloved, love, beautiful, vineyard, fragrance, dove.
Group: Wisdom Literature.
Audience: Israel.
Date: Maybe the 900s BC.
Popularity Rank: 46 of 66.

SONG OF SONGS

Lightning-Fast Summary: A joyous, sensuous, poetic celebration of love, marriage, and sex.

Unique Feature: At most, Song of Songs has one passing reference to God (8:6), and of all Bible books, it has the least overt theology.

Type of Book: Romantic poetry / love story.

So It's Just About Love and Attraction and Sex? Yep. It poetically describes five meetings between two lovers who go through all the dance steps of an intimate, romantic relationship. They yearn for each other, miss each other, their friends are abuzz about how they feel about each other, they very specifically express their attraction to each other, they marry each other, and they make passionate love to each other.

Is It All a Metaphor About Christ and the Church? Some smart people have argued for this, but go read it for yourself. It takes a lot of imagination to see this parallel in the actual text. There are other parts of the Old Testament that are explicitly fulfilled in the New Testament in ways that may not be obvious on your first read-through, but Song of Songs is never quoted or referenced in the New Testament. It looks like it really is just about love and sex.

It's Probably Best There's a Book That's Just About Love and Sex in the Bible: In the Wisdom Literature part of the Bible, we've seen a book about how things normally go in life (Proverbs), a book about unusual suffering (Job), and a book about malaise from unusual success and comfort (Ecclesiastes). It's important that the Bible speaks to all these aspects of life, and likewise, the Bible would be incomplete if it didn't speak to romance and intimacy in the language in which we experience it—a poetic love story.

What Does Song of Songs Teach Us to Do? Pretty much nothing. There aren't really any instructions in it. Rather, it models the value of love, intimacy, and commitment, and encourages the reader to understand love as a gift to be cherished and savored. The Lover and her Beloved are treated as right and good for being madly in love with each other, wanting to be married, and wanting to make passionate love together.

Who Wrote It? This book might be by King Solomon, or it might be in his honor. It's hard to say.

When It Was Written: Around the time of King Solomon (the 900s BC) is a good guess.

Tone and Feel: Passionate, pure, hopeful.

Important Characters: Solomon (who seems to be a far-off figure in the story), the Lover (Her), the Beloved (Him), and their Friends.

Original Language: Hebrew.

Original Audience: Israel in general, but most of all, lovers and anyone who loves love.

Parts of This Book That Kids Underline and Pass to Each Other While Giggling:

- "Your breasts are like two fawns, like twin fawns of a gazelle." (4:5)
- "His arms are rods of gold set with topaz. His body is like polished ivory decorated with lapis lazuli." (5:14)
- "Your stature is like that of the palm, and your breasts like clusters of fruit. I said, 'I will climb the palm tree; I will take hold of its fruit.'" (7:7–8)

Three Great Verses That Kind of Sum Up the Whole Thing:

- "I am my beloved's and my beloved is mine; he browses among the lilies." (6:3)

- "Many waters cannot quench love; rivers cannot sweep it away. If one were to give all the wealth of one's house for love, it would be utterly scorned." (8:7)
- "Let him kiss me with the kisses of his mouth—for your love is more delightful than wine." (1:2)

Theme Verse: Song of Songs 8:6—"Place me like a seal over your heart, like a seal on your arm; for love is as strong as death, its jealousy unyielding as the grave. It burns like blazing fire, like a mighty flame."

Theme: A beautiful celebration of love, attraction, marriage, and physical intimacy.

Unsung Hero: The group of friends who chime in from time to time. They all seem to be huge fans of love and are able to genuinely celebrate someone else's happiness.

Unsung Hero #2: God, who came up with the ideas of love, marriage, and sex and gave them to people as a lavish gift.

If You Don't Have Time to Read the Whole Thing, at Least Read: The final chapter, which neatly mirrors the tensions of the opening chapter and contains one of the most beautiful declarations of love in the whole Bible (8:6–7).

When You Visualize Song of Songs, Picture: Young lovers embracing.

VITAL STATS

Position: 23 of 66.
Chapters: 66.
Verses: 1,292.
Word Count: 25,608 (6/66).
Most-Used Words: Lord, God, Israel, people, nations, land, day.
Group: Major Prophets.
Prophesying To: Judah.
Date: Around 680 BC.
Popularity Rank: 6 of 66.

Lightning-Fast Summary: Through the prophet Isaiah, God pronounces judgment against disobedient Israel and the evil nations of the world but then makes promises about a future restoration and deliverance for all through the Messiah.

Genre Jump: If you're reading straight through the Bible, there's probably no more shocking change of pace and tone than the one that happens between Song of Songs and Isaiah. Song of Songs is a succinct, sensual love song seemingly separated from the larger story. But Isaiah is a prolonged, profound book of prophetic pronouncements against Israel and her neighbors coupled with promises about God's ultimate long-term plan to redeem.

Song of Songs marks the end of the Wisdom Literature section of the Bible, and Isaiah is the first of the Major Prophets.

How the Timeline Works: The first seventeen books of the Bible tell one massive story about the descendants of Abraham over a huge amount of time. There are a few side quests (like Ruth and Esther) and one big reset of the whole story (Chronicles), but it's all basically a single story told in order. The next five books (Job, Psalms,

Proverbs, Ecclesiastes, and Song of Songs) aren't chronological; rather, they're stories or compilations from all over the larger story of the first seventeen books. The final seventeen books of the Old Testament are all prophetic books in which God uses prophets to talk to Israel or their neighbors. These books happened between the early 700s BC and the mid-400s BC, and they're not arranged chronologically.

Who Were the Prophets? They were messengers of God who spoke to the people of Israel. Sometimes they predicted future things, but more often they spoke encouragement, correction, and even judgment to God's chosen people (and sometimes to others too).

Major Versus Minor Prophets: The Major Prophets are the long ones, and the Minor Prophets are the short ones. Isaiah, Jeremiah (and his second book, Lamentations), Ezekiel, and Daniel are considered the Major Prophets. Most of the prophetic books are directed at the Southern Kingdom of Judah and Jews in exile.

Unique Feature: Isaiah is sweeping in scope. He speaks to Judah in his time (the late 700s BC), Judah in the time of Babylon (the early 500s BC), as well as to the Jews who were to be restored under Persia (the late 500s BC). Isaiah also speaks of the redemptive work of God through the Messiah in the time of Christ.

One Unified Book in Three Books, Written to Three Audiences:

- The first third of Isaiah (chapters 1–39) contains prophetic warnings for the rebellious people of Israel in the 700s BC during the time of the Assyrian Empire. Isaiah warns the people to fear God instead of the nations and predicts that Babylon will one day take them into exile. These prophecies of judgment are a huge problem because they mean the end of the kingdom of David, yet the one who defeats the curse and reigns forever on David's throne is supposed to come from David. But in chapter 11, there's hope. The line of David's family is imagined as a burned-out stump. It looks dead, but then it sprouts a green shoot that represents the Messiah, descended from David, who will come and defeat the curse after all. God's judgment is coming for the kingdom of Judah in 586 BC, but His redemptive plan is still on.

- The second third of Isaiah (chapters 40–55) speaks to the exiled Jews in Babylon in the mid-500s BC and opens with the words, "Comfort, comfort my people, says your God. Speak tenderly to Jerusalem. . . ." God comforts His people by promising restoration for Israel, judgment for Babylon, and a yet-to-come "Suffering Servant" who will set things straight.
- The third part (chapters 56–66) is for everyone who follows God. It is very big-picture, and it looks to the distant future when God's redemptive plan is realized among all the nations and where God brings about a new heaven and a new earth in which all things are made right and the curse from back in Genesis is defeated.

Who Wrote It? The first verse of the book specifically names Isaiah son of Amoz as author and main human character. Chapter 1 places Isaiah in Judah from the mid-700s through the early 600s BC, and Isaiah makes appearances as a character in 2 Kings 19 and 20 and in 2 Chronicles 32. That's all pretty cut and dried.

However, Isaiah contains a bunch of very specific predictions about the future that nobody could have known (like specifically naming Cyrus as the guy who would one day defeat Babylon, 150 years in advance), so some people look at this and say that everything from chapter 40 to the end must have been written by later authors writing in Isaiah's name.

Buuuuuut Isaiah is a book of the Bible, and the Bible assumes God's total power over nature and time, and the book itself holds out God as showing Isaiah future things. The New Testament quotes Isaiah a ton and only ever credits him as the prophet responsible for the book that has his name on it. There's no indication in the Bible that anyone other than the original Isaiah son of Amoz wrote this book.

When It Was Written: Around 680 BC.

Original Language: Hebrew.

Tone and Feel: Stern, then compassionate, then wildly hopeful.

Important Characters: God continues to be the main character of the whole Bible, but you'll notice He's an exceptionally active and present character in Isaiah and many of the other prophetic books. Also Isaiah, Ahaz, Hezekiah, Cyrus the Great (king of Persia), and the Suffering Servant.

Isaiah Talks About Jesus a Lot: Isaiah doesn't make vague references to "maybe Jesus." They are explicitly about Jesus, and the New Testament overtly confirms that Isaiah is predicting Jesus' birth, life, death, and the salvation that will one day come through Him. Here are some famous examples:

1. "The virgin will conceive and give birth to a son, and will call him Immanuel." (Isaiah 7:14, which is quoted in Matthew 1:23 when Jesus is born)
2. "For to us a child is born, to us a son is given, and the government will be on his shoulders. And he will be called Wonderful Counselor, Mighty God, Everlasting Father, Prince of Peace. Of the greatness of his government and peace there will be no end. He will reign on David's throne and over his kingdom, establishing and upholding it with justice and righteousness from that time on and forever. The zeal of the Lord Almighty will accomplish this." (Isaiah 9:6–7, and really all of Isaiah 9, which are the lyrics to Handel's *Messiah*)
3. "But he was pierced for our transgressions, he was crushed for our iniquities; the punishment that brought us peace was on him, and by his wounds we are healed." (Isaiah 53:5, which is referenced in 1 Peter 2:24)
4. "The Spirit of the Sovereign Lord is on me, because the Lord has anointed me to proclaim good news to the poor. He has sent me to bind up the brokenhearted, to proclaim freedom for the captives and release from darkness for the prisoners, to proclaim the year of the Lord's favor and the day of vengeance of our God, to comfort all who mourn." (Isaiah 61:1–2)

But Are We *100 Percent* Sure These Are About Jesus? Yes. In Luke 4:21, Jesus literally goes to a synagogue, pulls out Isaiah, scrolls to that last verse just quoted, reads it aloud, and then says, "Today this scripture is fulfilled in your hearing."

The tomb of Cyrus the Great.
Petr/stock.adobe.com

But Are We *10,000 Percent* Sure? Still yes. In John 12:41, John specifically says that "Isaiah said this because he saw Jesus' glory and spoke about him."

The Suffering Servant: Chapters 52 and 53 have this beautiful prophetic song about a suffering servant (who turns out to be Jesus). These fifteen verses are quoted thirty-seven times in the New Testament. So it's a big deal.

Important Motifs: God's judgment, a glimmer of hope, the Messiah, defeating the curse, light in the darkness.

Theme Verse: Isaiah 1:18—"'Come now, let us settle the matter,' says the Lord. 'Though your sins are like scarlet, they shall be as white as snow; though they are red as crimson, they shall be like wool.'"

Theme: The zeal of the Lord will accomplish His redemptive plan for His glory.

If You Don't Have Time to Read the Whole Thing, at Least Read: The whole thing. I know it's long, but it's the summary of the plot and theology of the Old Testament in a nutshell, and it tees up Jesus and the New Testament perfectly. If you're really in a hurry, make sure you put eyes on 52:13–53:12 at minimum.

When You Visualize Isaiah, Picture: A green shoot coming out of a dead stump as a reminder that God will defeat the curse through the line of David, just as He promised.

VITAL STATS

Position: 24 of 66.
Chapters: 52.
Verses: 1,364.
Word Count: 33,002 (1/66).
Most-Used Words: Lord, God, land, people, house, king, Jerusalem.
Group: Major Prophets.
Prophesying To: Late-stage Judah.
Date: Early 500s BC.
Popularity Rank: 16 of 66.

JEREMIAH

Lightning-Fast Summary: Jeremiah tells Judah that they've prostituted themselves to fake gods for too long, and now God is going to wreck His own temple and the kingdom of Judah, using the Babylonians as His instrument of destruction. Despite all this, Jeremiah says God still has good plans for His people in the future.

Unique Feature: Jeremiah is the longest single book of the Bible by word count.

These Books Have Action: The prophetic parts of the Major Prophets are all interspersed with great action sequences. Jeremiah has plenty of gripping narrative, with real stakes for him as a character.

Who Wrote It? Overwhelmingly it's by Jeremiah, but he has an assistant named Baruch who helps him. Jeremiah is called the "weeping prophet" because he's in anguish over his people's failures and fate. Jeremiah has to watch it all come to pass with his own eyes in the last chapter of the book.

How It's Built: Jeremiah and his scribe Baruch assembled a bunch of material from Jeremiah's lengthy career, including narrative, prophecies, predictions, laments, and poems. Chapter 36 describes some of the process by which the book is built.

Jeremiah Is Out of Order: Jeremiah is not chronological. Instead, it's organized around theological themes.

When It Was Written: It describes events starting around 625 BC and wrapping up in 586 BC. It was finished up sometime after that.

Historical Setting: There's a moment right before the collapse of a kingdom or an empire when there's no saving it, but the people are in denial. Jeremiah is writing to that moment in the history of the Southern Kingdom of Judah, and the people who are lying to themselves about how things are going unsurprisingly loathe Jeremiah for telling them the truth.

What Truth? Jeremiah's message is that God has had enough. He'll no longer tolerate Judah's spiritual adultery. God's people have broken the covenant, but God is going to keep up His end of the deal by punishing them harshly.

Was It That Bad? Yes. One could smell the burnt incense to God near Solomon's temple and then walk a ways and smell the stench of child sacrifice to pagan gods down the street.

What Kind of Punishment Are We Talking About? Jeremiah prophesies that God will bring Babylon to destroy Jerusalem and the temple and take the people into captivity. That is to say, he predicted the complete destruction of Judah.

So Does That Make Babylon the Good Guys? Hard no. Babylon is the clumsy instrument God will deftly wield to execute His judgment. After that, God will judge and punish wicked Babylon as well (chapters 51–52).

Important Characters: God, Jeremiah, Baruch, King Zedekiah, Nebuchadnezzar, King Jehoiakim, a bunch of false prophets.

Villain: You'd think it would be Babylon, and that's sort of true, but the most corrupt bad guys in Jeremiah are the people in Judah who are in denial and lash out at Jeremiah—mocking and beating him, imprisoning him, kidnapping him, and throwing him into a cistern to sink into the mud and suffocate (chapter 38).

Tone and Feel: Regretful, lamenting rebuke, but also tender and hopeful at times.

More About the Hopeful Stuff, Please: Jeremiah's telling his own people that their world as they know it is about to end, and it's their own fault. But around the halfway point (chapters 29–33), Jeremiah makes it clear that even though there's no escaping Babylon, the Jews are going to get through it. God even puts a timeline on it. In Jeremiah 29:10, He says, "When seventy years are completed for Babylon, I will come to you and fulfill my good promise to bring you back to this place [Jerusalem]."

. . . And That's Exactly What Happened: Nebuchadnezzar conquered Jerusalem and made the Jews exiles in 586 BC, then Cyrus of Persia conquered Babylon and let the Jews go back to Jerusalem to rebuild the temple, which was completed and dedicated in 516 BC.

Seventy years. Just like God said through Jeremiah.

The Messiah: Remember Isaiah's imagery with the burned-out stump and the green shoot that grows up out of it to symbolize the restoration of the line of David? Well, Jeremiah draws on this language in chapter 23: "I [God] will raise up for David a righteous Branch, a King who will reign wisely and do what is just and right in the land. . . . This is the name by which he will be called: The Lord Our Righteous Savior" (vv. 5–6).

A New Covenant: In an Old Testament full of covenants, Jeremiah 31 envisions an entirely new one in the future. God says the days are coming when He will make a new covenant with His people that isn't like the one He made with their ancestors. In this new one, instead of writing the law on tablets and scrolls, He's going to write His law on their hearts, and then finally He will be His people's God, and they will be His people.

Unsung Hero: Faithful Baruch, who records and even publicly proclaims Jeremiah's hard-to-stomach prophecies.

Problematic Curse: In chapter 22, God declares that none of the descendants of evil King Jehoiachin (son of King Jehoiakim) will "sit on the throne of David or rule anymore in Judah" (v. 30). In this curse, God specifically says to Jehoiachin in verse 24 that if he "were a signet ring on my right hand, I would still pull you off."

This curse is a big problem because if God doesn't rescind it, then the Great Eternal King and Redeemer promised by God can't come from the line of David, and the whole redemptive plan might be canceled.

Around seventy-five years later, God lifts the curse when he tells Zerubbabel, who is directly descended from Jehoiachin and King David, that He will "make you like my signet ring, for I have chosen you" (Haggai 2:23).

Stuff You Can Still Physically Look At: The town of Anata (biblical Anathoth) was Jeremiah's hometown, and a few glimpses of the ancient settlement still remain.

Most Quoted Verse: Jeremiah 29:11—"'For I know the plans I have for you,' declares the Lord, 'plans to prosper you and not to harm you, plans to give you hope and a future.'"

Most Misunderstood Verse: Yeah, it's also Jeremiah 29:11. Jeremiah just gets done delivering God's promise to bring judgment and ruin on Judah, and now he's in the middle of a very specific prophecy where he's telling the exiled Jews to bear down and endure being a subjugated people working for the peace and prosperity of Babylon. This is an important theme verse of the book that speaks to God remembering Judah, but the context makes it a little less ideal candidate for an inspirational lower-back tattoo.

Reconstruction of the Ishar Gate at the ruins of Babylon, near modern Al-Hillah, Iraq.

rasoulali/Shutterstock.com

Most Relatable Moment: Jeremiah loves his own people. He tries to talk sense to them, but they're too far gone, and now he has to watch them buckle under the weight of their own folly. Surely every one of us has ignored warnings from people who love us, and surely every one of us has tried to help someone we love who's on a collision course with calamity.

A Book So Good They Made a Word Out of It: *Jeremiad* is a fancy word for a lamenting, righteous prophecy of doom.

Theme Verse: Jeremiah 3:12.

Theme: Crushing judgment is coming, but so is a new covenant.

If You Don't Have Time to Read the Whole Thing, at Least Read: The Messiah stuff in Jeremiah 29–33.

When You Visualize Jeremiah, Picture: A weeping prophet.

VITAL STATS

Position: 25 of 66.
Chapters: 5.
Verses: 154.
Word Count: 2,324 (39/66).
Most-Used Words: Lord, people, city, cry, destruction, daughter, enemies.
Group: Major Prophets.
Prophesying To: Freshly exiled Jews.
Date: 586 BC.
Popularity Rank: 54 of 66.

Lightning-Fast Summary: A collection of five grief poems, lamenting Jerusalem's destruction at the hands of the Babylonians in 586 BC.

Unique Feature: Four of the five poems that make up the book are acrostics, where each successive line of the poem starts with the next letter of the Hebrew alphabet.

Written Before the Dust Had Settled: Lamentations was composed while the shock of Nebuchadnezzar's destruction of Jerusalem was still fresh.

Who Wrote It? It's technically anonymous, but it's always been associated with Jeremiah. It sounds like him, and he was there to see with his own eyes the events that inspired these poems.

When It Was Written: Anytime after 586 BC, but go read it for yourself—not much time has passed for the author. These poems are raw. They sound like they're written by someone who can still smell the stench of death, feel the heat of the burned city, and see the dust kicked up on the horizon by the captives being marched away.

Original Audience: Stunned, grieving Jewish exiles, many of whom were probably there on that fateful day.

Tone and Feel: Gut-wrenching devastation over the loss of a place and a people.

Important Characters: There's a noticeable lack of characters in Lamentations, and this helps convey the ghost-town setting of ruined Jerusalem in the first verse of the book: "How deserted lies the city, once so full of people! How like a widow is she, who once was great among the nations!"

How It's Built: Each poem in Lamentations is one chapter long, and there's no bonus material at all. No introduction, no epilogue, just five poems. Full stop.

Symmetry: Every chapter but the middle one (chapter 3) has exactly twenty-two verses. The middle chapter, which contains the central idea, has sixty-six verses, or exactly three times the number of each of the other chapters.

Jerusalem in Ruins: The first poem is about the wreckage of the city. The grief fires in all directions—toward allies who never answered calls for help, toward Babylon, and toward the poet himself and the people for rebelling against God. The poet doesn't blame God; he acknowledges the judgment was just. But he wraps up the poem begging God to punish Judah's enemies with the same ferocity He showed in dealing with His chosen people's sin.

The Lord's Fierce Anger: Poem two is about God's pitiless fury poured out against His rebellious people.

Sober Reflection: Poem three is an expression of Judah's frustration and a reflection on the good character of God as a point of consolation.

Before and After: Poem four is a contrast between the glory of Jerusalem and its people when it thrived, and the soot and ashes after the Babylonians came.

Remember: Poem five is an appeal to God to remember His people and restore them to Himself.

Most Shocking Moment: In the second and fourth poems, there are lines describing how some mothers resorted to killing, cooking, and eating their own children during Nebuchadnezzar's siege.

What Would Happen If Lamentations Weren't in the Bible? It would be weird to just move on with the story without grieving it. This is the closest thing to the end of the world the original audience could imagine. It isn't just that they lost a war or had to move; everything they understand about the unfolding of history and their place in it has been shaken to the core. Jerusalem meant something to them, and it's meant something to us as the reader. If what happened here won't make you pause to grieve and reflect, nothing will.

Also, it's in the Bible to show that God is compassionate and right in His judgments, even in a moment like this.

Literally the Middle Verse of the Book: This might not be something to pay attention to in most books, but in one so tightly and mathematically structured, it probably matters. This verse is the central idea of a book about God's just judgment against His own people: Lamentations 3:32–33—"Though he brings grief, he will show compassion, so great is his unfailing love. For he does not willingly bring affliction or grief to anyone."

Most Famous Verse: Lamentations 3:22–23—"Because of the Lord's great love we are not consumed, for his compassions never fail. They are new every morning; great is your faithfulness."

The poet trusts the character of God, even after God brought crushing judgment on His own people.

Theme: Grief in the context of a compassionate God's righteous judgment.

If You Don't Have Time to Read the Whole Thing, at Least Read: The middle poem (Lamentations 3).

When You Visualize Lamentations, Picture: An empty throne and a broken crown.

VITAL STATS

Position: 26 of 66.
Chapters: 48.
Verses: 1,273.
Word Count: 29,918 (4/66).
Most-Used Words: Lord, Israel, house, house of Israel, land, people, son, Son of Man.
Group: Major Prophets.
Prophesying To: Jewish exiles.
Date: From July 31, 593 BC to April 26, 571 BC.
Popularity Rank: 26 of 66.

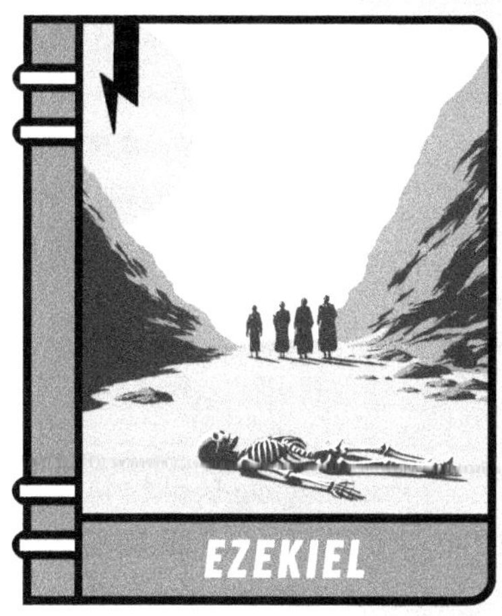

Lightning-Fast Summary: A collection of prophecies and stories from the long career of the prophet Ezekiel, who predicted Jerusalem's fall, was taken into exile, and continued to prophesy in Babylon.

Unique Feature: Ezekiel was a dramatic prophet who used tons of public performance art to communicate his prophecies in shocking and memorable ways.

A Foot on Either Side of the Divide: All four major prophets straddled two huge epochs in history. Isaiah was there for the fall of the Northern Kingdom and the eradication of ten of the twelve tribes of Israel at the hands of the Assyrian Empire. Jeremiah and Ezekiel both started their lives in the free kingdom of Judah and died as exiles. Daniel got his start in late-stage Babylon and lived out his days in the newly minted Persian Empire.

They all predicted that the writing was on the wall for the kingdoms they started out in, and they all continued to be faithful to God under their new overlords after the calamities they foretold came to pass.

Who Wrote It? Ezekiel, whom God calls Son of Man (Jesus will use that title for Himself later in the Bible).

What Do We Know About Him? A lot. His dad's name was Buzi. He was married, but his wife dies in chapter 24. Nebuchadnezzar took small batches of Jewish captives back to Babylon with him before he destroyed Jerusalem in 586 BC. Ezekiel (as well as Daniel) was among these preexilic exiles. Ezekiel was in his mid-twenties when he was taken in 597 BC. Later, when Ezekiel was thirty (specifically on July 31, 593 BC), he was sitting by a canal near Babylon when God appeared and commissioned him to be a prophet.

These Glorious Dates! No book of the Old Testament uses more specific time markers than Ezekiel. He uses days, months, and years relative to the reign of kings, so it's possible to nail down parts of the book to exact dates and days of the week.

How It's Built: Like Jeremiah, Ezekiel is a collection of stories, prophecies, and poems from across his twenty-two-year career. Ezekiel is more chronologically arranged than Jeremiah, but it still jumps around at times for thematic emphasis.

When It Was Written: The first entry is on exactly July 31, 593 BC, and the last entry is on April 26, 571 BC. All the entries were probably compiled and arranged very shortly after 571.

Historical Setting: At the beginning of the book, Nebuchadnezzar is tightening his grip on Jerusalem, and by the end of the book, Jerusalem is in ruins and the Jews are more than a decade into their time as Babylonian exiles.

Stuff You Can Still Physically Look At: If you go to Iraq, you can still see the outlines of ancient Babylonian canals like the one Ezekiel was sitting next to when God called him to be a prophet.

Who Ezekiel's Talking To: Even though Ezekiel addresses the people of the kingdom of Judah, he favors the name *Israel* for talking about God's chosen people around the time of the Babylonian conquest and exile. The old Northern Kingdom of Israel is long gone when Ezekiel is writing, so when he says *Israel,* he means descendants of Jacob, whose name had been changed to Israel.

Important Characters: God, Ezekiel, the house of Israel, Nebuchadnezzar, the prince of Tyre (an actual guy and a stand-in for all the proud rulers of the nations).

Villains: Those who oppose God—like the rebellious leaders of Judah, false prophets, and proud and corrupt foreign nations.

Tone and Feel: Intense and at times otherworldly but also underscored with hope for God's redemptive work to come.

Ezekiel Sees Angels: The book opens with Ezekiel sitting by a canal in Babylon. He's thirty years old, so he should be made a priest this year but instead he's in exile. But in an instant, God shows up riding a golden litter (one of those mobile throne things that servants carry on their shoulders) surrounded and supported by heavenly beings who sound like something out of a sci-fi movie. God tells Ezekiel that He is sending him to the Israelites, who are "a rebellious nation that has rebelled against me; they and their ancestors have been in revolt against me to this very day. The people to whom I am sending you are obstinate and stubborn" (2:3–4).

Parts You Might Recognize Even If You Haven't Read the Bible: Those angels have captured imaginations for twenty-five hundred years, including in recent years when the internet has been fascinated by the concept of biblically realistic angels.

The Ol' Judgment-and-Hope Combo: Just like Isaiah and Jeremiah, Ezekiel is a mix of judgment for Israel and the nations, as well as hope in the form of a future vision of God's deliverance. All these major prophets point to a short to midterm hope for the people of Israel, but they also point to an ultimate hope and complete redemption moment in the distant future in Jesus.

Performance Art Prophecy: Chapters 4–32 are mostly judgment, and as God predicted, the people aren't hearing any of it. Ezekiel tries to get through to them by doing prophetic performance art to illustrate what Israel has gotten wrong and what Israel has coming. Some of this art includes lying on his side for 390 days to represent 390 years of Israel's sin, making a clay model of Jerusalem to show how it will be destroyed, and baking bread over cow turd to show the Israelites what kind of unclean food they'll have to stomach when they get taken into exile.

God Leaves the Temple: In the middle of this section, there's one particularly troubling vision in chapters 8–11, where Ezekiel sees the cloud of God's presence leaving the temple and heading east toward Babylon. That cloud of God had been with them in the desert after the exodus, and God showed up in that way at the dedication of Solomon's temple. God had lived in the temple among His people for centuries, but now He's leaving. This is a very big moment in the unfolding of the Old Testament story.

The Clown-King Motif Is Back: From chapters 25–32, Ezekiel prophesies about the kings of the world who imagine themselves to be gods, but ultimately God will expose them all as impotent clowns (like all the haughty kings in the Bible). Ezekiel uses the prince of Tyre as the epitome of the clown-king.

Jerusalem Falls Again: Depending on how you count it, chapter 33 is the fifth or even sixth accounting in the Bible of the fall of Jerusalem at the hands of Nebuchadnezzar in 586 BC. That event left a mark.

The Dry Bones Come Back to Life: In chapter 34, God promises a future Shepherd who will search for His sheep and look after them (Jesus specifically calls himself "the good shepherd" in John 10:11).

Then in chapter 37, God takes Ezekiel to a valley with a bunch of long-dead corpses; only the dry bones are left. He tells Ezekiel to prophesy them back to life, and then God knits them all back together. God will bring Israel back to life, and He'll go a step further and defeat the curse of sin and death altogether through Jesus, six hundred years after Ezekiel.

The book wraps up with eight chapters of visions of what things will look like when God completes His redemptive plan and finally defeats the curse once and for all.

A Peek at God's Motives: In chapter 36, God makes it clear He isn't doing all this restoration because Israel will earn it through future exemplary behavior, but rather that He's going to redeem them for the sake of His own name. "It is not for your sake, people of Israel, that I am going to do these things, but for the sake of my holy name, which you have profaned among the nations where you have gone" (36:22).

Unsung Heroes: The remnant of Israel. That's what Scripture calls the people who stayed faithful to God through the whole mess.

Theme Verse: Ezekiel 36:26—"I will give you a new heart and put a new spirit in you; I will remove from you your heart of stone and give you a heart of flesh." This is echoed in 2 Corinthians 5:17: "Therefore, if anyone is in Christ, he is a new creation. The old has passed away; behold, the new has come" (ESV).

Theme: Judgment for Israel now, but hope for Israel and all creation later.

If You Don't Have Time to Read the Whole Thing, at Least Read: Ezekiel 34 about the future Shepherd and Ezekiel 37 about the valley of dry bones.

When You Visualize Ezekiel, Picture: Dry skeletons coming back to life.

The traditional site of Ezekiel's Tomb in Al Kifl, Iraq.

Farhadmirza/CC BY-SA 4.0

VITAL STATS

Position: 27 of 66.
Chapters: 12.
Verses: 357.
Word Count: 9,001 (26/66).
Most-Used Words: God, king, Daniel, dream, vision, kingdom, Nebuchadnezzar.
Group: Major Prophets.
Prophesying To: Jewish exiles in Babylon and Persia.
Date: Late 500s BC.
Popularity Rank: 35 of 66.

DANIEL

Lightning-Fast Summary: The story of a faithful Jewish prophet in exile who interprets dreams and survives dangerous political times in Babylon and Persia.

Unique Feature: Of all the Old Testament books, Daniel is the one that speaks most directly to the era in between the Old and New Testaments. It's the only book in the Old Testament that explicitly mentions Greece, and chapters 8 and 11 seem to predict Alexander the Great's conquest of Persia in the 330s BC.

Who Wrote It? Christian and Jewish tradition say Daniel is both the main character and the author. With remarks He makes in Matthew 24:15, Jesus confirms that Daniel wrote at least part of the book of Daniel.

Bonus Surprise Writer: Nebuchadnezzar, the scourge of Jerusalem himself, is held out as the author of a good chunk of chapter 4.

What We Know About Daniel: He was a remarkable talent of noble birth who caught the eye of King Nebuchadnezzar, who was in the habit of deporting promising young men to Babylon long before the fall of Jerusalem. In keeping with the admonition of Jeremiah to "seek the peace and prosperity of the city to which I have carried you into exile" (Jeremiah 29:7), Daniel effectively served kings in Babylon from 605 BC until the first year of Cyrus the Great of Persia (around 538 BC).

How It's Built: The first half is mostly narrative, in the style of the Old Testament historical books, and the second half is mostly apocalyptic prophecy, predicting future events. Because of this organization, the events in the book aren't always arranged chronologically.

When It Was Written: Christians and Jews traditionally believe it was written by Daniel in the late 500s BC.

Historical Setting: Like all the Major Prophets, the book of Daniel spans a world-changing conquest. Daniel starts in the era of Babylon, but in chapter 5, Cyrus the Great of the Medo-Persian Empire defeats Babylon, and Daniel lives out the rest of his days in Persia.

Original Audience: Jewish exiles in Babylon who were looking to the future.

Type of Book: Apocalypse, with historical, theological narrative.

Tone and Feel: Daniel's storytelling has an optimistic tone; trusting in God more than kings and kingdoms.

Daniel's prophetic chapters feel much different than Isaiah, Jeremiah, and Ezekiel. While those three look forward with hope, they also spend a ton of time looking backward to prophecy about what went wrong with God's chosen people. Daniel doesn't look back at the old failings of the Jews; instead, he looks to the future. Daniel's prophecies range in time from the near term in the ancient world all the way out to the completion of God's redemptive plan at the end of history.

Stuff You Can Still Physically Look At: The ruins of Babylon are still visible in Iraq, and there is a tomb purported to be Daniel's in Susa, Iran.

Important Characters: Daniel, Shadrach, Meshach, Abednego, Nebuchadnezzar, Belshazzar, Darius the Mede, Cyrus, Michael.

Parts You Might Recognize Even If You Haven't Read the Bible: In the first half of the book, Daniel and three of his friends get taken from

Jerusalem to Babylon, and God helps them perform well there, even giving Daniel the ability to interpret dreams. Eventually Daniel's friends run afoul of Nebuchadnezzar when they refuse to worship a statue of him, and they get thrown into a fiery furnace. But God protects them, and they emerge unharmed. The dreams, the furnace incident, and a period of God-induced humiliation make an impression on Nebuchadnezzar, and he writes about the glory and power of the God of Israel. Daniel later gets sold out by jealous bureaucrats, and the king sentences him to death in a lion pit. But God shows up again, and Daniel is spared.

The Prophecy Part of the Book: The tone and style of the book totally change after chapter 6. Daniel relays visions that accurately predict how the ensuing half millennium of geopolitics plays out. He predicts the fall of Babylon, the fall of Persia to Alexander the Great, the death of Alexander and the distribution of his empire, the Jewish Maccabean revolt, and the rise of the Roman Empire. Even skeptical scholars who think Daniel might have been written as late as the early 100s BC can't account for how far into the future Daniel is able to see with clarity.

At the end of the book, Daniel looks even further ahead, to the very end of time, when God completes His redemptive plan.

Daniel's Vision of Jesus: In 7:13–14, Daniel says, "I looked, and there before me was one like a son of man, coming with the clouds of heaven. He approached the Ancient of Days and was led into his presence. He was given authority, glory and sovereign power; all nations and peoples of every language worshiped him. His dominion is an everlasting dominion that will not pass away, and his kingdom is one that will never be destroyed."

Most Controversial Part: At the end of chapter 9, Daniel issues the prophecy of the seventy "sevens" or seventy weeks. It's a cryptic timeline prophecy that's sparked tons of debate over the centuries.

Most Shocking Moment: When a disembodied hand appears at an indulgent king's banquet in Babylon and starts writing messages of doom on the wall. Babylon, which seemed too big to fail, is defeated that very night.

Unsung Hero: The archangel Michael, who fights off a demon nicknamed "the prince of the Persian kingdom" to deliver a message to Daniel.

Theme Verse: Daniel 2:44—"In the time of those kings, the God of heaven will set up a kingdom that will never be destroyed, nor will it be left to another people. It will crush all those kingdoms and bring them to an end, but it will itself endure forever."

Theme: God is the Master of history, the true eternal King, and He will guide history to His redemptive ends.

If You Don't Have Time to Read the Whole Thing, at Least Read: Daniel 1 and 6.

When You Visualize Daniel, Picture: Daniel surrounded by relaxed lions.

The foundations of Nebuchadnezzar's palace (possible site of the writing on the wall incident), Babylon.

VITAL STATS

Position: 28 of 66.
Chapters: 14.
Verses: 197.
Word Count: 3,615 (36/66).
Most-Used Words: Lord, Ephraim, Israel, God, people, love, king, Judah, Egypt, days.
Group: Minor Prophets.
Prophesying To: The Northern Kingdom of Israel.
Date: 715 BC.
Popularity Rank: 45 of 66.

HOSEA

Lightning-Fast Summary: Hosea's terrible marriage to his unfaithful wife is a metaphor for Israel's unfaithfulness in her relationship with God.

Unique Features: Only three of the seventeen books of prophecy in the Old Testament are directed at the Northern Kingdom of Israel, and Hosea is one of them. Also, Hosea is positioned first among the books of the Minor Prophets.

The Minor Prophets: The Minor Prophets are the fifth and final subdivision of the Old Testament after the Law (the Five Books of Moses), the Histories, the Wisdom Books, and the Major Prophets. During the time between the Testaments, the Jews lumped the Minor Prophets into one scroll called "the Twelve Prophets" and organized them roughly by era, so they're sort of in chronological order, but not quite.

What Makes Them Minor? It's not the content. What they have to say is hyperimportant to the unfolding of the Bible. It's just that they're way shorter than the Major Prophets. The average word count of the books named for the four major prophets is a whopping 24,000 words, whereas the average word count of the Minor Prophets is only 1,800.

Who Wrote It? Hosea son of Beeri, who prophesied to the Northern Kingdom of Israel for roughly thirty-five painstaking years. Everything we know about him is from this book.

Who Is Ephraim? Ephraim is the title Hosea uses for the Northern Kingdom of Israel, because it was the largest and most important of the ten tribes that made up the Northern Kingdom.

Historical Setting: Hosea is set during the final days of the Northern Kingdom, and it describes a dumpster fire, the likes of which we haven't seen since Judges. Israel is adrift, like a twig carried by a current (10:7). Six kings come and go in the final quarter century of Israel, and four of those get murdered during the time they sit on the throne. The specter of the bloodthirsty Assyrians looms large, and the kings in the North have no clue how to deal with this threat. One of them tries bribing the Assyrians to be merciful with tribute, others try sacrificing to idols, and another (Hoshea) tries rebellion. The Assyrians don't take kindly to that. In 722 BC, they destroy the Israelite capital of Samaria and deport and disperse the ten tribes of Israel.

The Northern Kingdom put nineteen kings on the throne over the course of its 210-year existence, and not a single one of them was good. They spiraled into wicked injustice and vile moral insanity and got wiped from history by Assyria.

Tone and Feel: Accusatory and satirical.

Stuff You Can Still Physically Look At: The ruins of Samaria, where you can still see evidence of what the Assyrians did there.

Important Characters: Hosea, Gomer, Jezreel, Lo-Ruhamah, Lo-Ammi.

Hosea's Difficult Call from God: God tells Hosea he has to marry a "promiscuous woman" (1:2) named Gomer and have kids with her. They have three, and God makes Hosea give them names that communicate God's anger toward Israel. Gomer is an unfaithful wife, and God uses that as a metaphor for the unfaithfulness of Israel, but then God makes Hosea go and buy her back from another man she sold herself to. God says that's a metaphor for how God will one day restore His faithless people at His own expense.

Reaping the Whirlwind: Throughout most of the rest of the book (Hosea 4–10), God enumerates the adulterous sins of Israel. They are many, and they are ugly. God calls them out for societal injustice, grotesque idolatry to basically any false god they hear about, faithless leadership, disregard for the covenant, and foolhardy dependence on treaties with other nations to save them. God is having Hosea tell the people to repent, but it's pretty clear they're not going to do that. At one point, God coins a famous phrase describing Israel: "They sow the wind and reap the whirlwind" (8:7). The sharp, even satirical tone of correction in these chapters is reminiscent of when God shows up to talk to Job and tells him to "brace yourself like a man" (Job 38:3).

Somehow There's Always Hope at the End: Since early in the Old Testament, God has been saying that if His people return to Him, He'll forgive them and restore them, and He says it again in the closing chapters of Hosea.

Most Shocking Moment: God makes Hosea knowingly enter into a marriage with a faithless wife.

Jesus Comes Up: Hosea 11:1 says, "And out of Egypt I called my son." It seems innocuous enough, but Matthew 2:15 says that this prophecy is fulfilled in Jesus, who was in Egypt as a child while Herod was looking to kill Him.

Theme and Theme Verse: God doesn't want His people to go through the perfunctory paces of a sham marriage with Him; He wants their hearts. This comes through in Hosea 6:6—"For I desire mercy, not sacrifice, and acknowledgment of God rather than burnt offerings."

If You Don't Have Time to Read the Whole Thing, at Least Read: Hosea 1–3 and 11.

When You Visualize Hosea, Picture: Hosea buying back his wife.

VITAL STATS

Position: 29 of 66.
Chapters: 3.
Verses: 73.
Word Count: 1,447 (51/66).
Most-Used Words: Lord, people, God, land, nations, great, wine, grain, locusts.
Group: Minor Prophets.
Prophesying To: Judah.
Date: Hard to say.
Popularity Rank: 56 of 66.

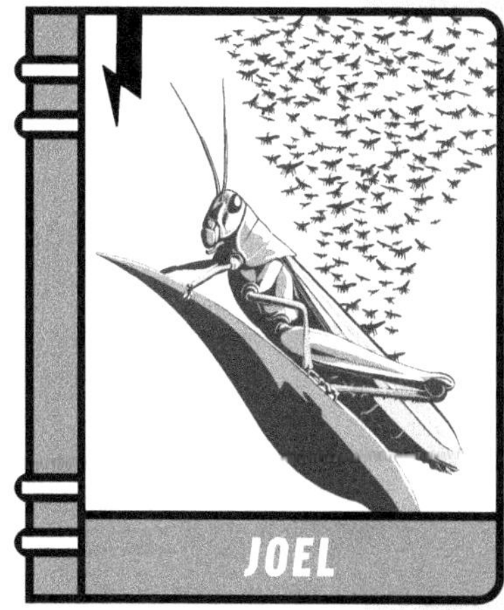

JOEL

Lightning-Fast Summary: Joel points to a horrible locust plague that ravaged Judah as a wake-up call from God meant to prepare His people for the coming "day of the Lord" (Joel 1:15).

Unique Feature: Joel doesn't give us any specifics about when these locusts came or when he was writing. Guesses range from the 800s BC all the way up to the time of Alexander in the 300s BC, and everywhere in between.

Unique Feature That Doesn't Spotlight a Bug: It would be weird to have a book like Daniel, with tons of specific prophecy, presented with an ambiguous time frame. For that book to make sense, Daniel needs to be in a certain place and time. But for Joel and his timeless message about some future glorious reckoning he calls "the day of the Lord," it works better thematically that he could be writing at almost any time.

Who Wrote It? Verse 1 says it was Joel son of Pethuel. Christians and Jews have always attributed it to him, and in Acts 2, Peter specifically credits Joel as the author of this book when he quotes Joel 2:28–32.

Historical Setting: Some sort of calamity has recently befallen the Southern Kingdom of Judah (or maybe Jews after the exile in and around Jerusalem), and the people are grieving, regrouping, and trying to make sense of what it means.

Tone and Feel: Like a horror film about a swarm of bugs, but then full of life and optimism after the bugs leave.

Waves Upon Waves of Locusts: Joel asks the people if anyone has ever seen anything like what they've just lived through. Locusts came and ate almost everything, then there was a fresh hatch, and the young locusts picked over what was left, then some other swarms blacked out the sky and ravaged whatever meagerly remained. There's no food for the people and nothing for the livestock. What isn't dead soon will be.

It Gets Worse: In chapter 2, Joel imagines the locusts as a grotesque human army descending on Jerusalem. He calls it the day of the Lord.

What Is the Day of the Lord? It's a terrifying reckoning of God when evil, injustice, and corruption finally get judged. The day of the Lord isn't a onetime thing. This specific idea comes up in most of the prophetic books across a bunch of historical settings. Sometimes God's chosen people are on the receiving end of the day of the Lord (as in the first part of Joel), sometimes it's the wicked nations facing the day of the Lord, and eventually it will be all evil, injustice, and corruption that God crushes on the ultimate day of the Lord to come.

There's Always Hope: Joel opens with a dark day of the Lord, then seems to predict another. But in the second half of the book, Joel foretells a great day of the Lord when God says He will "pour out my Spirit on all people" (2:28). The book ends with a vision of God's judgment of the nations (another day of the Lord) and the realization of a future reality where God lives with His people with justice and glory.

Most Shocking Moment: The graphic imagery of the plague.

Most Famous Verses: Joel 2:13–14—"Rend your heart and not your garments. Return to the Lord your God, for he is gracious and compassionate, slow to anger and abounding in love, and he relents from sending calamity. Who knows? He may turn and relent and leave behind a blessing."

The Holy Spirit Comes Up: In the New Testament, Peter draws a straight line from Joel 2 to the arrival of the Holy Spirit on the day of Pentecost (a day of the Lord, in a sense?), recorded in Acts 2.

Theme: The great and terrible day of the Lord.

When You Visualize Joel, Picture: All those locusts.

VITAL STATS

Position: 30 of 66.
Chapters: 9.
Verses: 146.
Word Count: 3,027 (37/66).
Most-Used Words: Lord, Israel, declares, land, house, sovereign, people, fortress.
Group: Minor Prophets.
Prophesying To: Mostly the Northern Kingdom of Israel.
Date: 750ish BC.
Popularity Rank: 52 of 66.

AMOS

Lightning-Fast Summary: The Northern Kingdom of Israel is at its apex of power and wealth, but it's made them fat and happy and guilty of tons of social injustice. God sends Amos, a shepherd from Judah, to call them out for it.

Unique Feature: Amos is among the very oldest prophetic books, and maybe the first to pronounce the judgment of God against His own people instead of against other nations.

Who Wrote It? Amos, a shepherd/farmer from a town called Tekoa in Judah.

When It Was Written: Around 750 BC.

Historical Setting: Amos's king was Uzziah of Judah, who also went by Azariah. Until Uzziah wobbled at the very end, he was a solid king who ruled for fifty-two years and brought stability to Judah from 792–740 BC. Up north in Israel, the king was Jeroboam II, who reigned for forty years from 793–753 BC. Despite being prideful and idolatrous, Jeroboam II expanded the borders of Israel, had huge economic success, and presided over the golden age of the North. Second Kings 14 explicitly credits God for what went right during this time.

He Just Wanted to Farm Figs: Usually, when we meet a prophet in the Old Testament, they get introduced as So-and-So Son of So-and-So. It's an indicator of esteem and fame. But Amos gets introduced as "Amos, one of the shepherds of Tekoa" (1:1). He doesn't even get called the *best* shepherd from the tiny town of Tekoa. He's not descended from priests or prophets; he's just an okay shepherd who also farms figs. He's the very epitome of *some guy*.

Sent to Israel: Amos prophesies a couple of sentences in passing about his home country of Judah, but oddly enough, God plucks this poor fellow out of his quiet life and sends him to the neighboring kingdom of Israel with a message of judgment to a people who've become comfortable and lax toward God.

Nobody's Laughing Now: The first several short prophecies of Amos are against the enemies of Judah and Israel. These have a fun cadence to them, where each neighboring nation gets a two-sentence message of judgment that starts with, "For three sins of [insert your godless country here], even for four, I will not relent. Because . . ." And then it says why God is judging them.

These were probably a ton of fun for the people of Israel to hear. But then Israel's giggling stops in chapter 2 when Amos turns and points the prophetic finger at them.

God's Complaint Delivered by Amos: Once Amos starts calling out Israel, he never stops. For seven chapters, he calls them out for corruption, false worship of God, and most of all, he calls them out for their cruel injustice during a time of great prosperity. Among many other things, Amos bawls them out for using dishonest scales against the poor (8:5), charging obscene taxes (5:11), and taking poor people's garments as security for a debt and then lounging on their clothing while their impoverished owners shiver (2:8). Amos isn't vaguely griping about a general notion of unfairness or ranting about the perceived inconsistencies of his political opponents; rather, he's pointing to tons of specific points of cruelty and exploitation that are in violation of God's laws, like the compassionate law that says you have to give someone's coat back at night so they can use it to sleep in (Deuteronomy 24:12–13).

Ruins and caves near ancient Tekoa.

Todd Bolen/BiblePlaces.com

Israel Isn't Having Fun, and They'd Like Amos to Leave Now: Eventually, Israel has had enough, and Amaziah the priest of Bethel (in Israel) yells at Amos, telling him to go back to Judah and make his dirty prophecy money there. Amos fires back, pointing out that he'd rather be home farming figs and that, unlike Amaziah and his ilk, Amos is speaking true prophecies, not false ones in exchange for money. Then Amos is like, "Hey, speaking of true prophecies that might rub people the wrong way, here's one from God for *you*, Amaziah," and then Amos literally says (conveying the Lord's message), "Your wife will become a prostitute in the city, and your sons and daughters will fall by the sword. Your land will be measured and divided up, and you yourself will die in a pagan country. And Israel will surely go into exile, away from their native land" (7:17).

We don't hear anything else from Amaziah after that.

There's Always Hope: After nine long chapters of judgment, culminating in Amos's accurate prediction of Israel's doom, the final five verses offer hope. In Amos 9:11, God says, "In that day, I will restore David's fallen shelter—I will repair its broken walls and restore its ruins—and will rebuild it as it used to be."

Plumb Line: Every prophet has a unique, memorable visual, and for Amos, it's a plumb line (a weighted tool that uses gravity to make sure a wall is straight and true).

Theme Verses: The plumb line stuff is in 7:7–8, where it says, "The Lord was standing by a wall that had been built true to plumb, with a plumb line in his hand. And the LORD asked me, 'What do you see, Amos?' 'A plumb line,' I replied. Then the Lord said, 'Look, I am setting a plumb line among my people Israel; I will spare them no longer.'"

Tone and Feel: Unrelenting prophecy of calamity, with only a few moments of hope tagged on at the very end.

Most Famous Verse: Amos 5:24—"But let justice roll on like a river, righteousness like a never-failing stream!"

Theme: God blessed Israel with unmerited prosperity, and they used it to exploit the weak—now judgment is coming.

When You Visualize Amos, Picture: A plumb line.

VITAL STATS

Position: 31 of 66.
Chapters: 1.
Verses: 21.
Word Count: 440 (63/66).
Most-Used Words: Lord, Esau, house, possess, mountains, disaster, people, nations.
Group: Minor Prophets.
Prophesying To: Edom.
Date: Probably mid-500s BC.
Popularity Rank: 66 of 66.

OBADIAH

Lightning-Fast Summary: An oracle about the destruction of Edom.

Unique Feature: Obadiah is the shortest book of the Old Testament, and the least searched Bible book on the internet.

Why It's in the Bible: Throughout the Old Testament, God is protective of His own name and reputation. When the Israelites obey Him, He blesses them so everyone will know He's the one true God, but when Israel disobeys Him, God often uses godless foreign nations to punish His own people so that, either way, everyone will know He's the one true God. However, He doesn't want to give the impression He's pleased with those other nations, so He always remembers to punish them for their wickedness as well.

At one level, Obadiah is in the Bible to make it clear that God didn't forget about the offenses of the Edomites. On a second level, Obadiah is in the Bible to point to a future restoration for Judah.

Who Wrote It? Obadiah is a common name in the Old Testament, and this Obadiah probably isn't the same guy as any of the others we've read about.

When It Was Written: Probably in the mid-500s BC, but some smart people think it's much older

Historical Setting: Verse 12 reads, "You [Edom] should not gloat over your brother in the day of his misfortune, nor rejoice over the people of Judah in the day of their destruction." So that supports the theory that Obadiah's prophecies are happening shortly after Babylon wrecks Jerusalem in 586 BC.

Obadiah gives the impression that the Edomites may have even marched with Babylon against Israel. It says, "You should not march through the gates of my people in the day of their disaster . . . nor seize their wealth in the day of their disaster" (v. 13).

Who Edom Is: Edom is an ancient kingdom on the southern end of the Dead Sea. They're the descendants of Esau, who was the son of Isaac and the brother of Jacob. Back in the middle section of Genesis, Jacob swindles Esau out of Isaac's blessing. This sets in motion the story that includes Jacob having his name changed to Israel and being the father of the sons for whom the tribes of Israel are named. In the end, Esau turns out to be a decent chap, but his descendants the Edomites are a thorn in the side of Israel for centuries. So because Edom is a cousin people group to Israel, it's extra awful when they abuse and mock God's chosen people.

The Day of the Lord: God's day of reckoning is coming for Edom, and eventually all the wicked nations, according to verse 15: "The day of the Lord is near for all nations. As you have done, it will be done to you; your deeds will return upon your own head." The final verses of Obadiah make it clear that God has plans to restore His people after Edom is knocked down from her lofty perch.

Wait, That's It? Where's the Part Where Judah Gets Criticized? Obadiah is the rare prophet who doesn't speak oracles of judgment against Judah or Israel. This book is all bad for Edom, and all good for Judah.

Tone and Feel: Fiery and personal.

Theme Verses: Obadiah verse 13 sums up the charges against Edom very thoroughly (quoted above), and the final verse (v. 21) sums up the hope for Judah and the establishment of God's kingdom: "Deliverers will go up on Mount Zion to govern the mountains of Esau. And the kingdom will be the LORD's."

Theme: Edom and all the nations that oppose God will be judged, and God will establish His kingdom.

When You Visualize Obadiah, Picture: Edom.

VITAL STATS

Position: 32 of 66.
Chapters: 4.
Verses: 48.
Word Count: 1,082 (56/66).
Most-Used Words: Lord, Jonah, God, sea, Nineveh, city, great, vine, die.
Group: Minor Prophets.
Prophesying To: The Northern Kingdom of Israel and Assyria.
Date: Mid-700s BC.
Popularity Rank: 57 of 66.

Lightning-Fast Summary: A reluctant prophet gets called to preach to the terrifying Assyrians in Nineveh. Instead of going there, he flees by ship and gets tossed into the sea, where he's swallowed by a huge fish. He survives, and his low-effort preaching in Nineveh is well received, much to his chagrin.

Unique Feature: Jonah is the least cooperative prophet in the Bible.

Who Wrote It? It's anonymous (although Jonah surely provided the story).

When It Was Written: The story is set during the reign of Jeroboam II, who was in charge from 793–753 BC. It was probably written down shortly after.

Time Covered: A few months or longer.

Structure: Jonah is a tidy book. It's got four chapters that each represent one movement in the story.

Tone and Feel: It has whimsy and irony, and Jonah is the butt of the joke. The irony is that the prophet of God tends to be faithless, while the godless outsiders are the ones who turn to and believe in God, first on the ship and then in Nineveh.

Historical Setting: In 2 Kings 14, Jonah prophesies to King Jeroboam II of the Northern Kingdom of Israel that God will be with him as he goes to war to restore Israel's old boundaries. Jonah turns out to be right, and Israel enters a golden age. But Jeroboam II isn't grateful to God; instead, idolatry and gross social injustice go unchecked on his watch. Instead of bringing Jonah back, God takes a different route and calls on a Judean fig farmer with no reputation (that's Amos) to come up and speak God's judgment against the king. While all of this is going on, the threat of the Assyrian Empire looms large.

Nineveh: For a long time, critics of the Bible surmised this city was exaggerated in size, confused with some other ancient city, or made up altogether, but in the nineteenth century AD, it emerged from the sands of time right where it was supposed to be. The discovery proved Nineveh was huge and well-fortified, just as the Bible describes it. God Himself calls it a "great city" and tells Jonah to go there and "preach against it, because its wickedness has come up before me" (1:2).

The Boat Scene: Jonah knows that God's assessment of Nineveh is right, and he wants nothing to do with it, so Jonah runs in the opposite direction, hops a ship, and sails for the far ends of the earth. Unsurprisingly, God, who knows everything, isn't fooled, and He sends a storm to redirect Jonah. Everyone on board fears for their lives. Jonah demonstrates some character and admits he's the problem and volunteers to be thrown overboard to appease God. The pagan sailors throw Jonah in the water and plead with God for forgiveness and deliverance. It works. The sea grows calm.

The Fish Scene: But that's not it for Jonah. God sends a huge fish (not a whale) to swallow Jonah whole. For three days, Jonah is in there, and he composes a beautiful prayer/psalm of repentance and gratitude. Then the fish barfs him up on dry land.

In this book, Jonah is at his best when he's in the fish.

The Streets of Nineveh Scene: Jonah goes to Nineveh and spends another three days going through the city, saying only, "Forty more days and Nineveh will be overthrown" (3:4). This feels like the passive-aggressive bare minimum on his part. He doesn't say anything about what they got wrong or who would do the destroying or how to avert this calamity.

Yet somehow it works.

The people repent, and the king issues a decree requiring everyone to ask for God's forgiveness. "Who knows?" the king says. "God may yet relent and with compassion turn from his fierce anger so that we will not perish" (3:9).

God is happy with that and decides to spare them.

The Tantrum Scene: God might be happy, but Jonah's not. He gripes at God for sparing them. "That is what I tried to forestall by fleeing to Tarshish," Jonah moans. "I knew that you are a gracious and compassionate God, slow to anger and abounding in love, a God who relents from sending calamity. Now, Lord, take away my life, for it is better for me to die than to live" (4:2–3).

Jonah had set up camp outside the city to watch its destruction, and God had even caused a miraculous shade plant to grow to help Jonah be more comfortable while he eagerly anticipated the doom of Nineveh. Jonah liked the plant, but then God sent a worm to eat the whole thing. God asks Jonah if it's right for him to be so mad about the plant and the worm, and Jonah says, "It is . . . and I'm so angry I wish I were dead" (4:9).

Then God says, "You have been concerned about this plant, though you did not tend it or make it grow. It sprang up overnight and died overnight. And should I not have concern for the great city of Nineveh, in which there are more than a hundred and twenty thousand people who cannot tell their right hand from their left—and also many animals?" (4:10–11).

And Then That's the End of the Book: Seriously. That's it. The reader is left to twist in the wind with Jonah and try to make sense of it all.

In the End, Nineveh Still Gets Judged: Nineveh forgot about God and reverted to what it'd always been. They never repented again, and God used Babylon and the Medes to crush Nineveh in 612 BC. The book of Nahum celebrates this as the just judgment of God.

Nebi Yunis, tomb of the prophet Jonah, not far from Nineveh, Iraq.

Public domain

Most Shocking Moment: Getting swallowed by a fish and living inside it for three days was probably less shocking to the original audience than the idea of the Assyrians repenting and trusting God.

Jonah 3:5 reads, "The Ninevites believed God." That phrase is the signature trait of Abraham, the man of faith, about whom it was said, "Abram believed the LORD, and he credited it to him as righteousness" (Genesis 15:6). In chapter 3 of the book of Galatians in the New Testament, the apostle Paul says that non-Jews who put their trust in Christ are following in the faith footsteps of Abraham and are saved along with him.

Jesus Points to Jonah: In Matthew 12, Jesus likens Jonah's time in the fish to the time He'll spend in the grave. He also compliments the Ninevites for repenting.

Jonah's Right About This One Thing: Jonah said that God is "gracious and compassionate" and "a God who relents from sending calamity," though it may not seem that way as you read the words of the prophets, who condense all of God's judgments against these ancient kingdoms down to a few pages. But if you think about how patient God was and how much "not judgment" happened in the vast majority of the evil times described in the Old Testament, you can see that Jonah has a point. But the other side of the judgment coin is justice. Justice for the victimized. Justice for the oppressed.

God holds Himself out in the Bible as doing exactly the right amount of justice through judgment at exactly the right times for His redemptive purposes.

This can be understandably hard for the reader to wrap their head around.

Theme Verses: Jonah 4:2 and 4:10–11 (quoted earlier).

When You Visualize Jonah, Picture: The huge fish, representing God's judgment, justice, and mercy all at once.

VITAL STATS

Position: 33 of 66.
Chapters: 7.
Verses: 105.
Word Count: 2,118 (42/66).
Most-Used Words: Lord, people, God, Israel, Zion, Jacob, nations, house.
Group: Minor Prophets.
Prophesying To: Israel and Judah.
Date: Maybe around 700 BC.
Popularity Rank: 50 of 66.

Lightning-Fast Summary: Micah warns Israel and Judah to humble themselves and start being just and merciful, or they're going to end up in exile. But whether they clean up their act or not, God will still see His redemptive plan through.

Unique Feature: Micah and Isaiah both prophesy at the same time, and there's a ton of overlap between the two. Isaiah's prophecies are framed with the noble court in mind, while Micah speaks to the common folk.

Who Wrote It? Micah is a book of the prophecies of the prophet Micah (obviously), but as is the case with a lot of the books in this section, it's hard to say whether the prophet himself assembled the book in its final form or whether someone else took his prophecies and formed them into the collection we read today. Either way, Christians believe the process was inspired by God.

What Do We Know About Him? Micah, like Amos, was from a little village in Judah—Moresheth—and didn't run in fancy circles. He had a soft spot for the lowly and oppressed. He wasn't familiar with the royal court and the halls of power like Isaiah was. Furthermore, we don't get an account of how he became a prophet, and his own book never even formally calls him by that title (though Jeremiah does later on). Instead, Micah credits his authority to "the Spirit of the Lord" in 3:8.

Years Covered: Micah is prophesying about stuff happening in Judah during the reigns of Jotham, Ahaz, and Hezekiah (those three reigns ran from 750–687 BC). He was probably only active intermittently during that time frame. The book of Micah itself may have come together around 700 BC.

Historical Setting: After the economic and military golden age of Jeroboam II (782–753 BC) in the Northern Kingdom of Israel, things spiraled toward collapse quickly. Just thirty years after Jeroboam II died, Assyria conquered Israel and deported her people into historical oblivion. Micah predicted Israel's fall in 1:6. When Micah started his work, both kingdoms still existed, and when he finished, only Judah remained.

Israel, the Cautionary Tale: To Micah, it's simple. Israel was idolatrous and unjust, and her fate is sealed. Now Judah has a choice to make. She can repent of those same offenses or face the fate of Israel.

Tone and Feel: Micah has bite. He uses satire and wordplay to drive home his critiques.

Structure: Micah's prophecies are grouped in four cycles of judgment and restoration. It's not chronological, and the judgment sections are longer.

The Judgment Half of the Four Cycles: Rich people in Judah have discovered a clever way to exploit poor people. They wait for a couple of bad harvests to happen, and then instead of helping the people out, these ghouls swoop in and buy up families' ancestral land when they're going through tough times. This flies in the face of God's law (Numbers 36:7), and it ruins the idea of God's chosen people being uniquely just as a way to show outsiders who God is. Micah rails against injustices like these and against the corruption of the leadership. He says judgment will come from foreign empires if the people don't turn back to God.

The Restoration Half of the Four Cycles: God says He'll shepherd His people and show love to Jacob and Abraham as He promised long ago (2:12–13 and 7:14–20). In Micah 4 and 5, God also says (and this is one of the most important things in the whole book) that there's going to be a glorious far-off future when evil is crushed and all nations come to Jerusalem to worship God, and there'll be perfect justice and perfect provision for everybody, and there'll be no more war. Again, and this cannot be stressed enough, these promises are for *all nations*, not just Judah. Outsiders will be part of this blessing in the last days, fulfilling what God promised to Abraham in Genesis 12:3: "All peoples on earth will be blessed through you."

Jeremiah Approves: About a hundred years later, Jeremiah affirms Micah as a prophet and quotes Micah 3:12 in Jeremiah 26:18: "Micah of Moresheth prophesied in the days of Hezekiah king of Judah. He told all the people of Judah, 'This is what the Lord Almighty says: "Zion will be plowed like a field, Jerusalem will become a heap of rubble, the temple hill a mound overgrown with thickets."'"

Most Shocking Moment: Jeremiah quotes these words to the people of his day just before the Babylonians arrived and did to Jerusalem exactly what Micah had predicted a hundred years earlier.

Micah Points to Jesus: Seven hundred years after all this, Magi from the east show up in the court of Herod the Great, asking where to find the newborn king of the Jews. Herod doesn't know, so he calls in his religious experts, who reference Micah 5:2: "But you, Bethlehem, in the land of Judah, are by no means least among the rulers of Judah; for out of you will come a ruler who will shepherd my people Israel" (Matthew 2:6). Herod believes Micah's prophecy and sends the Magi to Bethlehem, where they find Jesus and his family.

Most Applicable Moment in the Entire Old Testament: By the time you get to Micah, all that has been laid out in the Old Testament can feel overwhelming. There's so much evil and injustice, and worst of all, some of the things the prophets call out hit a little too close to home. It's humbling, and it raises the question, "How do I get it right?" Any softhearted reader who's moved by the mistakes of Israel and Judah is begging for God to simplify it all and just tell us what to do by this point in the Bible. And in Micah 6:8, we get an answer.

Theme Verse: Micah 6:8—"He has shown you, O mortal, what is good. And what does the LORD require of you? To act justly and to love mercy and to walk humbly with your God."

Theme: God will judge His people for acting unjustly, despising mercy, and acting proudly. But He's planning a future restoration for His people and for the nations, where His justice and mercy will reign forever.

When You Visualize Micah, Picture: The manger scene in Bethlehem.

VITAL STATS

Position: 34 of 66.
Chapters: 3.
Verses: 47.
Word Count: 855 (59/66).
Most-Used Words: Lord, Nineveh, chariots, locusts, city, fire, mountains, prey, plunder, water.
Group: Minor Prophets.
Prophesying To: Judah and Nineveh.
Date: Late 600s BC.
Popularity Rank: 63 of 66.

Lightning-Fast Summary: God will destroy Nineveh and the Assyrians.

Unique Feature: Nahum resolves questions left unanswered by Jonah.

This Book Is Simple: Nahum predicts the fall of Nineveh (and with it, the reviled Assyrian Empire).

Who Wrote It? Nahum of Elkosh. That's everything we know about him.

Historical Setting: Assyria was the worst empire ever, and everyone was sick of her. In 612 BC, the Babylonians and Medes destroyed the Assyrian capital of Nineveh and effectively ended the Assyrian empire.

Years Covered: Nahum is writing before the fall of Nineveh in 612 BC but after the fall of Thebes in 663 BC (which he mentions in chapter 3). That means he was probably prophesying during the reign of good King Josiah of Judah (640–609 BC).

Tone and Feel: Resolute in righteous judgment and vividly creative in its description of Nineveh's day of reckoning.

Nineveh After Jonah: When Jonah reluctantly preached to Nineveh, they repented and God spared them. That made Jonah mad, in part because he was being childish but also because he knew how horrible Assyria and Nineveh had been to God's people, and he wanted God to unleash His wrath on them. He wanted justice for the atrocities and injustices over the centuries. Ultimately, God decided the day of reckoning for Nineveh would be delayed.

Over the next 150 years, Nineveh reverted to what it had always been, and then God judged them.

A Psalm of Praise to Open a Book of Woe: The first eight verses are a song celebrating the glory of God, His habit of delivering those who trust in Him, and His wrath against evil.

It Won't Be Assyria Who Comes for Judah: The rest of chapter 1 says that Assyria's days as the tormentor of Judah are over.

Nineveh Overrun: Chapters 2 and 3 colorfully describe the fall of Nineveh. God enumerates their evil. They have no future.

Nahum Resolves a Lot: Most of the prophetic books so far say that God is deftly going to wield the dull objects that are the nations to judge Israel and Judah. But every prophet who says something like that also says that God is then going to judge those nations He uses to punish Israel. In Nahum, we finally see those warnings realized. God used Assyria to judge Israel, and now Assyria and Nineveh, her great capital, will be judged for their evil.

Nahum Might Seem Harsh: But no matter how horrible you imagine Assyria to be, they were probably worse. In the same way there was a giant ticker-tape parade in New York to celebrate beating Hitler in World War II, so the entire ancient world would feel elation at the demise of the oppressor that loomed over them for three hundred years. If you're an American, imagine being violently oppressed for longer than the United States has existed. Assyria finally got a taste of its own medicine, and no one was sad about it.

Does Nahum Point to Jesus? No. It's pretty much just about Nineveh getting obliterated.

Most Applicable Moment for Modern Audiences: The reader is supposed to gloat a little over the fall of evil Nineveh, but at some point, the reader is also supposed to reflect on their own screwed-up stuff and repent of it.

Theme Verses: Nahum 1:7–8—"The Lord is good, a refuge in times of trouble. He cares for those who trust in him, but with an overwhelming flood he will make an end of Nineveh."

Theme: The judgment of God is terrifying, but that judgment is a function of His justice. God gives justice by crushing evil and delivers those who take refuge in Him.

When You Visualize Nahum, Picture: Nineveh and its demise.

VITAL STATS

Position: 35 of 66.
Chapters: 3.
Verses: 56.
Word Count: 1,011 (57/66).
Most-Used Words: Lord, nations, earth, sea, woe, though, net, violence, glory, God.
Group: Minor Prophets.
Prophesying To: Judah.
Date: Late 600s BC.
Popularity Rank: 55 of 66.

Lightning-Fast Summary : The prophet Habakkuk asks God why He let Judah become so evil, and why God is using an even more evil nation to punish His own people.

Then God answers Habakkuk. Habakkuk is satisfied and praises God.

Unique Feature: In most of the prophetic books, God has a prophet bring His objections against a nation. But in Habakkuk, the prophet brings his objections to God.

Who Wrote It? Habakkuk. He's mentioned twice in this book but nowhere else in the Bible, and we don't get any details about his life. There's also a fun legend about him helping Daniel while he was in the lions' den, but nothing concrete. In this book, he likens himself to a watchman on the wall.

Historical Setting: Habakkuk was prophesying in the very late 600s BC, just as Assyria was facing her final defeat. Jeremiah's career was in full swing at that time, and his memorable public proclamations said what most people knew but few were ready to admit out loud—Babylon is coming, and Judah's days are numbered. Habakkuk knew Jeremiah's message was from God, and it's even possible Habakkuk was in the streets of Jerusalem prophesying the same stuff at the same time as Jeremiah.

Type of Book: It's a respectful but pointed dialogue between Habakkuk and God. His questions are hard but humble, and God listens and answers directly.

Making Sense of Suffering: Habakkuk asks God to help him understand why evil has gone unchecked in Judah and why great suffering is coming down the pike. Job and his friends asked similar questions of God under different circumstances.

Tone and Feel: Brave, honest, and direct.

Question One: Habakkuk asks God why He hasn't done anything about Judah's evil; or all evil for that matter.

God's First Answer: God says, "I am doing something about the evil. I'm bringing Babylon to put an end to lots of it by crushing Judah" (paraphrase is mine—His full answer is in Habakkuk 1:5–11).

Question Two: Habakkuk asks God why He's using Babylon, since they're even more evil than Judah. After Habakkuk is done asking, he says, "I will stand at my watch and station myself on the ramparts; I will look to see what he will say to me" (2:1).

God's Second Answer: God says He'll punish Babylon for their own evil. Then He rests His case, saying, "The Lord is in his holy temple; let all the earth be silent before him" (2:20).

Habakkuk's Content with That: Habakkuk has no further questions, and the final chapter is a humble, trusting, poetic prayer calling on God for mercy for His people and judgment and justice for evil.

The Future Kingdom: In His second answer to Habakkuk, God talks about the same far-off, future kingdom that Micah pointed to a couple of books earlier. It's one in which all the world seeks God. In 2:14, God says, "For the earth will be filled with the knowledge of the glory of the Lord as the waters cover the sea."

Most Applicable Moment for Modern Audiences: At some point, everyone has wanted to ask God why and have Him answer us directly. Habakkuk actually got to do it. We might not get the chance to have such a conversation, but Habakkuk did, and after that experience, he came away trusting God more, even in the face of nearly unimaginable evil and suffering (a lot like Job).

Theme Verse: Habakkuk 2:4 (which is quoted in Romans 1:17; Galatians 3:11; Hebrews 10:38)—"See, the enemy is puffed up; his desires are not upright—but the righteous person will live by his faithfulness."

Theme: God is just and merciful and right, even when we don't understand what He's doing.

When You Visualize Habakkuk, Picture: A watchman on the wall.

VITAL STATS

Position: 36 of 66.
Chapters: 3.
Verses: 53.
Word Count: 1,141 (54/66).
Most-Used Words: Lord, land, people, live, declares, son, gather, seek, anger, remnant, but, wrath, city.
Group: Minor Prophets.
Prophesying To: Judah.
Date: 630 BC, give or take ten years.
Popularity Rank: 60 of 66.

Lightning-Fast Summary: Zephaniah says a fire of judgment and purification from God is coming for Judah and her neighbors.

Unique Feature: Zephaniah was the great-great grandson of King Hezekiah of Judah. He may not have been in line for the throne, but that pedigree put him squarely in the royal family, and that's not where prophets usually came from.

Who Wrote It? Zephaniah, who clearly knows his way around the royal court. He understands the structure of government with enough sophistication to notice and call out subtle procedural evils and white-collar injustices.

Historical Setting: Zephaniah was a part of the court of King Josiah, who was probably his cousin. Josiah reigned from 640–609 BC, which means Zephaniah prophesied at the same time as Jeremiah, Nahum, and Habakkuk. Josiah rediscovered the Book of the Law and led religious reforms, but Judah was too entrenched in idolatry and injustice to make the changes stick.

Type of Book: It's a good old-fashioned judgment and restoration prophetic book.

Tone and Feel: Refined, poetic, and weighty.

The Darkest Prophecy So Far: Wow. Zephaniah opens with a prophecy of comprehensive, creation-wide judgment. It sounds like God is threatening to undo creation with fire. Even Judah, the last remnant of God's people, won't be spared. Judah has reached a level of corruption that can't be fixed by kings, courts, or politics. God says a day of hot judgment is coming soon for Judah and her nobles and court officials, and their silver and gold won't save them. Zephaniah writes, "In the fire of his [God's] jealousy the whole earth will be consumed, for he will make a sudden end of all who live on the earth" (1:18).

God's Burning Anger Against Evil: In chapter 2, several nations are listed and indicted for their evil. Zephaniah describes the judgment that's coming and urges Israel to "seek righteousness, seek humility; perhaps you will be sheltered on the day of the Lord's anger" (v. 3).

Friendly Fire: In chapter 3, Zephaniah goes after his noble peers and the religious leaders in Jerusalem. He calls them defiled oppressors, roaring lions, wolves, unprincipled, and treacherous. He says they do violence against the law of God. They're unrepentant of any of it, and God is going to pour out His wrath on them and consume them "by the fire of my jealous anger" (v. 8).

Purification by Fire: The twist to this book comes in 3:9, when Zephaniah reveals that the fire of God isn't going to consume everything, leaving nothing behind. Rather, it is going to refine everything, purge evil, and bring true worshipers from every nation (including the scattered of Israel): "Then I will purify the lips of the peoples, that all of them may call on the name of the Lord and serve him shoulder to shoulder. From beyond the rivers of Cush my worshipers, my scattered people, will bring me offerings" (vv. 9–10).

A Dramatic Swing in Just Three Chapters: Zephaniah starts out by saying what everyone already knows—Jerusalem, the nations, and humanity in general are a complete mess. Evil abounds. Most of the leaders actually seem to enjoy the way things are. But by the end of the book, there's a solution in view. God will defeat evil with a justice so hot that the evil will melt away like dross, and what will be left will be a purified people with a new heart and a new spirit (like Ezekiel envisions in chapter 36 of his book). It's a vision of God's future kingdom.

Most Shocking Part: The talk of judgment in this book is sweeping and frightening. Most people want God to bring about justice, but when we actually think about what it would look like for God to purify things by exacting His full judgment against us, it's horrifying.

This Begs For Another Way: By the time we get to the end of the Old Testament, here's what's clear:

- The curse and the human problem are horrible and have to be fixed.
- Humans can't fix it.
- God's judgment against evil is needed, but what would be left if He really let loose?
- There has to be another way if we're to survive God's defeating of the curse.
- Someone else is going to have to endure God's wrath on our behalf.

We're Very Ready for Jesus: The Old Testament tees up the New Testament. Jesus is the perfect and only solution to the problem.

Most Famous Verse: Zephaniah 3:17—"The Lord your God is with you, the Mighty Warrior who saves. He will take great delight in you; in his love he will no longer rebuke you, but will rejoice over you with singing."

Theme Verse: Zephaniah 3:9—"Then I will purify the lips of the peoples, that all of them may call on the name of the Lord and serve him shoulder to shoulder."

Theme: God will judge with a purifying fire that will refine and restore His people.

When You Visualize Zephaniah, Picture: A crucible full of pure, refined, liquid metal.

VITAL STATS

Position: 37 of 66.
Chapters: 2.
Verses: 38.
Word Count: 926 (58/66).
Most-Used Words: Lord, almighty, declares, house, son, Haggai, people, Zerubbabel, twenty.
Group: Minor Prophets.
Prophesying To: Returning Jewish exiles in the Persian Empire.
Date: Late 520 BC.
Popularity Rank: 62 of 66.

Lightning-Fast Summary: Haggai tells the returning exiles to quit worrying about their own fancy houses and get back to work on God's house.

Unique Feature: All five prophecies that make up this book have exact dates attached to them. We know the precise day, month, and year on which every single thing in this book happened.

Who Wrote It? Haggai, who seems to have partnered with Zechariah (the guy who wrote the next book of the Bible).

When It Was Written: From late August through mid-December in 520 BC.

Type of Book: Motivational prophecy.

Tone and Feel: Kick-in-the-pants.

Historical Setting: God used Babylon to judge Judah in 586 BC when Nebuchadnezzar destroyed the temple and took God's people into exile. Then, just as He promised, God used Persia to punish Babylon in 539 BC. One year later, Cyrus the Great of Persia let the Jews go back to Jerusalem to rebuild the temple, exactly as Isaiah predicted in chapters 44 and 45. The book of Ezra tells the story of a direct descendant of David named Zerubbabel, who led the exiles home and began rebuilding. But after Zerubbabel finished laying the foundation in 538 BC, he ran into opposition, and the project stalled out until the time when Darius was king of Persia (522–486 BC). By the time of Haggai, the temple project had been back-burnered without progress for nearly twenty years.

Priorities: On August 29, 520 BC, God tells the Jews (through Haggai) to "give careful thought to your ways" (1:5). Though the temple has remained untouched for two decades, the Jews in Jerusalem have still somehow found time to build fancy paneled houses for themselves in the latest Persian style. God is not impressed and tells them to pay attention to His house, starting right now.

Zerubbabel (who would be king of Judah if there were still a kingdom) responds to prophetic correction like his royal ancestor King David did in the days of old and obeyed God. Just twenty-three days after Haggai's oracle, Zerubbabel and the men of the city are back to work.

Four More Oracles: Haggai prophesies four more times in chapter 2 (on September 21, October 17, and twice on December 18). He pushes the Jews to be strong and hold nothing back from the project. He shares with them a vision of the future glory of the temple that will be visible to all nations.

Finally, during what we call the Advent season, God singles out Zerubbabel and tells him about a coming day of the Lord and says He will make Zerubbabel "like my signet ring" (2:23).

This is a huge deal because it signals that God's plan to establish an eternal king from the line of David is still on. Jeremiah records a scary moment, eighty years earlier, when God rejects and curses one of the last kings of Judah by telling him that his offspring won't sit on David's throne and that even if that king were a signet ring, God would take it off (Jeremiah 22:24–30). The last verse of Haggai has God reversing that curse because of Zerubbabel's faithfulness and God's zeal to redeem.

What Happened After? Zerubbabel and the exiles completed the temple in 516 BC, and Zerubbabel's name went on to be among those in the genealogy of Jesus in Matthew 1.

Greater Glory Than the Last Temple: In Haggai 2, God says He will fill this new temple with glory that is more glorious than Solomon's. That comes true when Jesus goes to this new temple five-hundred-plus years later.

Theme Verse: Haggai 1:8—"Go up into the mountains and bring down timber and build my house, so that I may take pleasure in it and be honored."

Theme: God wants His house built, and He promises new and greater things to come in it.

When You Visualize Haggai, Picture: Fancy paneled houses next to the half-built temple in Jerusalem.

Excavations at Ramat Rachel.

Todd Bolen/BiblePlaces.com

ZECHARIAH

VITAL STATS

Position: 38 of 66.
Chapters: 14.
Verses: 211.
Word Count: 4,855 (33/66).
Most-Used Words: Lord, almighty, Jerusalem, house, Judah, angel, land, nations.
Group: Minor Prophets.
Prophesying To: Returning Jewish exiles in the Persian Empire.
Date: Finished around 480 BC.
Popularity Rank: 43 of 66.

Lightning-Fast Summary: Zechariah pushes the Jews to complete the second temple because it points to the Messiah and God's rule over all the nations.

Unique Feature: Zechariah is the minor prophet who feels most like a major prophet because of the chapter count and sweeping vision of the future, including the work of the coming Messiah.

Who Wrote It? Zechariah son of Berekiah, who was born an exile in Babylon. He learned to be a priest there and then made his way to Jerusalem after Persia conquered Babylon and let the Jews return to rebuild Jerusalem. He spoke to a lot of the same stuff as Haggai, but his career as a prophet lasted much longer.

When It Was Written: The last entries to this book probably happened during the reign of Xerxes, who features heavily as the king in the book of Esther. Xerxes was king of Persia from 486–465 BC.

Type of Book: Prophetic dreams and visions with some poetry.

Tone and Feel: Optimistic call to repentance in keeping with what the Lord will do in the future.

Historical Setting: Babylon destroyed Jerusalem in 586 BC and took the Jews into exile, but Persia conquered Babylon in 539 and allowed the Jews to go rebuild Jerusalem. It went well at first, but then the project bogged down. In 520 BC, God sent the prophets Haggai and Zechariah to get the returning exiles to finish building God's temple.

Time's Almost Up: When Jeremiah wrote in the late 600s BC, he said Babylon would take God's people into exile, but after seventy years they'd be restored (Jeremiah 25; 29–31). When Zechariah arrives in Jerusalem and begins prophetically urging the Jews to hurry up and build the temple, there are only a few years left before Jeremiah's predicted seventy years are up. Clearly Zechariah (and Haggai) believes that finishing that temple is the completion of the seventy-year prophecy.

What's Next: Zechariah spends a ton of time on what it's going to look like when God finally brings resolution to all those glimmers of hope from across the prophetic books.

Zechariah Throws Down the Gauntlet: Chapter 1 opens with Zechariah challenging the returning Jewish exiles of 520 BC to choose differently than their ancestors who ignored the prophets and never repented. Just look where that got them, he says. Zechariah prophesies in verse 3, "'Return to me,' declares the Lord Almighty, 'and I will return to you.'"

The people listen and repent.

Seven Weird Dreams: From the middle of chapter 1 through the end of chapter 6, Zechariah has seven prophetic dreams full of vivid imagery, including four horsemen, a woman flying in a basket, a lampstand, and a man with a line who measures Jerusalem. These seven visions mostly raise questions about the future of God's redemptive plan and the role Israel is going to play in it. God says the generation of exiles who are rebuilding the temple are pivotal in that plan and have to obey and play their part. These visions point to the Messiah and a future where all the nations—not just Jews—come and worship God. God says in 2:10–11, "'Shout and be glad, Daughter Zion. For I am coming, and I will live among you,' declares the LORD. 'Many nations will be joined with the LORD in that day and will become my people.'"

Repent, for the Kingdom of Heaven Is Near: In the second half of the book, the people are starting to get the idea of the importance of the Messiah and His kingdom, and Zechariah urges them to obey God and start to live by the values of that kingdom.

A Glimpse of a World Without the Curse: The closing chapters are stuffed with prophecies about Jesus, the coming Messiah. Zechariah envisions this coming future King riding into Jerusalem on a donkey in victory. He also envisions a Good Shepherd who gets rejected by His own flock. He's struck, and His sheep scatter.

Eventually the people realize they were wrong to reject the Shepherd, and they all mourn and repent. Zechariah describes it like this: "They will look on me, the one they have pierced, and they will mourn for him as one mourns for an only child, and grieve bitterly for him as one grieves for a firstborn son" (12:10).

Finally, Zechariah prophesies the judgment of the evil of the nations, but also the reign of God over all the people groups of the world.

So Much Jesus: The New Testament refers to Zechariah several times, and pretty much all of those references have to do with Jesus and His kingdom. Zechariah predicted several of the most poignant images from Jesus' life. Matthew even links the thirty pieces of silver and the potter's field referenced in Zechariah 11:13 to Judas's betrayal of Jesus (27:9–10).

At this point, the Old Testament is aching for Jesus.

Theme Verses: Zechariah 9:9–10—"Rejoice greatly, Daughter Zion! Shout, Daughter Jerusalem! See, your king comes to you, righteous and victorious, lowly and riding on a donkey, on a colt, the foal of a donkey. I will take away the chariots from Ephraim and the warhorses from Jerusalem, and the battle bow will be broken. He will proclaim peace to the nations. His rule will extend from sea to sea and from the River to the ends of the earth."

Theme: Repent, for the Messiah and His kingdom are near.

When You Visualize Zechariah, Picture: The Shepherd King.

VITAL STATS

Position: 39 of 66.
Chapters: 4.
Verses: 55.
Word Count: 1,320 (52/66).
Most-Used Words: Lord, almighty, God, covenant, offerings, Israel, great, faith, hands, curse.
Group: Minor Prophets.
Prophesying To: Jews living in rebuilt Jerusalem in the time of Persia.
Date: 450 BC or later.
Popularity Rank: 51 of 66.

MALACHI

Lightning-Fast Summary: Malachi prophesies against the sins of Jerusalem after Ezra's and Nehemiah's reforms.

Unique Feature: Malachi is the last book of the Old Testament and almost surely the last one to be written.

Who Wrote It? Malachi, but we don't get any biographical details on him.

When It Was Written: All we know for sure is that Zerubbabel's temple is already built when he's writing, so it has to be after 516 BC. That said, the books of Ezra and Nehemiah are ultra specific about what kind of sin and silliness the Jews fell into in the mid-400s BC, and everything those two guys were concerned about is the same stuff Malachi is concerned about. With that in mind, 450 BC or later seems like a good guess.

Type of Book: Corrective prophecy.

Tone and Feel: Heart-heavy that the people's faithlessness persists after all that God has done.

Historical Setting: After Babylon conquered Jerusalem, then Persia conquered Babylon, and then Persia let the exiles go to rebuild Jerusalem, there was a great generation of faithful Jews led by Zerubbabel, a descendant of David.

Sure, they needed a little prodding from Haggai and Zechariah, but they got the temple built, dedicated themselves to serving God, and looked forward to God accomplishing His redemptive plan.

After that, there was a crisis when Persian King Xerxes's right-hand man tried to kill all the Jews, but Queen Esther thwarted that, and the Jews continued to rebuild themselves as a thriving people of God. During the reign of Xerxes's son Artaxerxes, Israel's old enemies started skulking about, and Nehemiah was dispatched to Jerusalem to rebuild her walls. Shortly afterward, Ezra the priest returned as well. Ezra and Nehemiah were sickened to discover that the people were already repeating the same mistakes that landed them in exile in the first place, and they teamed up to lead a national repentance and renewal of the covenant. The reforms were painstaking for them and for the people, but everyone agreed they couldn't repeat the sins of their ancestors ever again.

Nehemiah went back to his job in Persia's capital, and when he returned years later, he found that Jerusalem was quickly relapsing into the sins he had just purged, including marrying foreigners who worshiped idols, neglecting the temple, and ignoring the Sabbath.

Malachi Wants the People to Honor the Covenant: Ezra, Nehemiah, and Zechariah knew the big picture of God's story and had internalized God's character. They understood that their moment represented one last chance to get it right, so they pulled out all the stops and set up the people and the temple for long-term success. Malachi was a prophet in that same tradition and with the same mindset: *We've got to get this right this time around.*

After centuries upon centuries of failure, these prophets wanted to see their people finally honor their covenant with God.

Malachi's List: Malachi starts out by reminding the people of God's faithfulness and love for them, despite all their mistakes. Then he takes a chapter (and a bit more) to describe their current unfaithfulness, and his list looks a lot like Ezra's and Nehemiah's.

Malachi says the priests have neglected to teach the law (something Ezra prioritized highly), the Jewish men are marrying foreign women who worship foreign gods, the rich are cheating the poor, and the people aren't tithing to support the temple.

The Remnant: Malachi envisions a scroll of remembrance on which God writes down the names of the faithful remnant who obeyed Him when their neighbors did not.

What's Next? The tone of the final page of Malachi's book isn't optimistic. You don't get the impression the people will listen and repent. Through Malachi, God promises a coming judgment for the wicked, but He also promises to send a new Elijah "before that great and dreadful day of the LORD comes. He will turn the hearts of the parents to their children, and the hearts of the children to their parents" (4:5–6).

John the Baptist Is This Elijah: In Matthew 11:14, Jesus explicitly states that John the Baptist is this Elijah who was promised at the end of Malachi, and he came to prepare the way for Jesus. In the same vein, Mark gives a nod to Malachi 3:1 when it says, "I will send my messenger ahead of you, who will prepare your way—a voice of one calling in the wilderness, 'Prepare the way for the Lord, make straight paths for him'" (Mark 1:2–3).

The State of Things: In many ways, we end the Old Testament on another trip around the loop we've seen since the beginning, where God blesses His people, then they get lazy and rebel, then He punishes them, then they repent, then He blesses them again, then they get lazy and rebel again, and on and on and on and on. Those last good generations produced great leaders like Zerubbabel, Haggai, Zechariah, Esther, Mordecai, Ezra, Nehemiah, and Malachi. They did everything they could to break the cycle, but even within their own lifetimes, they could see it wouldn't be enough.

The curse is too powerful to be broken by human effort alone. The Old Testament leaves off begging for God to intervene to save humanity and break the curse by His own power and at His own expense.

Jesus is up next, and the payoff is fantastic.

Theme Verse: Malachi 4:2 (which is the inspiration for the third stanza of "Hark! The Herald Angels Sing")—"But for you who revere my name, the sun of righteousness will rise with healing in its rays. And you will go out and frolic like well-fed calves."

Theme: Israel fails. All of humanity fails. But God doesn't, and redemption is coming.

When You Visualize Malachi, Picture: Malachi the prophet, sitting at his desk exhausted.

BETWEEN THE TESTAMENTS

Getting Our Bearings: Around 450 years have passed since Malachi prophesied in the last book of the Old Testament. That's the biggest time jump between consecutive books in all of Scripture.

Kind of a Lot's Happened Since Then: When we left off, the Persians were in charge, and the Jews were trying to obey God as a people. A hundred years after Malachi, in 332 BC, Alexander the Great marched on Jerusalem. The Jews welcomed him, and he offered sacrifices to God at the temple. Alexander went on to conquer Persia before dying in 323 BC. Three big Greek-like kingdoms emerged from his conquests and dominated the ancient world.

Mosaic of Alexander the Great found at Pompeii, Italy.

giannimarchetti/Shutterstock.com

Later, one of those empires conquered Jerusalem and outlawed Judaism. The Jews revolted in 167 BC and established an independent kingdom that lasted for a hundred years. This kingdom had the same problems as the Old Testament kingdoms of Israel and Judah, and in 63 BC, the Roman Republic took control. They set up the Herod family as puppet rulers in Judah. In the coming decades, Rome endured a civil war and morphed into an empire. The first emperor, Caesar Augustus (27 BC–AD 14), called for a census of his empire that prompted Mary and Joseph to go to Bethlehem, where Jesus was born.

Is God in the Temple? When Solomon dedicated the first temple, God showed up in the form of fire from heaven and a dark cloud that took up residence there. Just before Babylon destroyed the first temple, Ezekiel had a vision of the cloud of God's presence leaving the temple. In 516 BC, when the second temple was dedicated, that cloud never appeared.

Despite that, the Jews never went back to idolatry after the time of Ezra and Nehemiah in the mid-400s BC, and future generations of Jewish leaders put serious thought into building out a more thorough version of the law to make sure the people would never even get close to breaking the law given by Moses. Despite all the effort, the miraculous presence of God never visibly returned to the temple, and when the Roman general Pompey took control of Jerusalem in 63 BC, he strolled right into the holiest part of the temple and did not encounter the glory and presence of God.

What Now? By the time of Jesus, the Jews were a subject people group yet again, and God didn't seem to be living in the temple—all of that despite the Jews' best sustained effort to be pious and ritually pure. As the Old Testament wraps up, God's people are wondering, *When will God save? How will God save? What do we have to do?*

Geography and Politics Update: Rome gradually divided up her empire into provinces and often let local ethnic rulers help govern on her behalf. At the time of Jesus, Jerusalem was in the Roman province of Judea, which would later be famously governed by

Pontius Pilate. Jesus was born in Bethlehem in Judea, but his family was from Nazareth in Galilee. Galilee was smaller and simpler than bustling Judea, and it was also under Roman rule, even though it wasn't a full-fledged province. Most of Jesus' life and ministry happened up north in Galilee, where Herod Antipas was king.

Temple Upgrades: The big name in the Herod family was Herod the Great, who reigned in Judea from 37 to 4 BC. He built fortresses and public works all over Judea and hugely expanded the temple in Jerusalem. When he was done adding on to Zerubbabel's temple, it was even bigger and more immaculate than Solomon's temple that got destroyed by Babylon.

Jerusalem Under Roman Occupation: After being passed around between seven different kingdoms in the five hundred-ish years before Christ, the people splintered into several groups, with a variety of strategies for how to deal with Rome and how to move forward as a people in general.

Strategy Number 1—Retreat: Groups like the Essenes moved to the desert, lived disciplined lives, and dedicated their lives to the Scriptures and to ritual purity. These are the people who made the Dead Sea Scrolls, and John the Baptist had a lot in common with them.

The caves of Qumran, where some of the Dead Sea Scrolls were found.

Strategy Number 2—Appease: The Herod family was Idumean, not Jewish, but they found favor with the Roman court and ended up ruling over the Jews. The Herods needed to keep tax revenues flowing and prevent insurrection in order to hold on to their Roman-backed throne. Many Jews resented the Herods, but others reluctantly allied with them. Members of this pro-Herod Jewish political sect were called Herodians.

Strategy Number 3—Play the Game: A Jewish council of religious leaders called the Great Sanhedrin governed the temple. The Sadducees were the dominant political party there, and they cooperated with Rome, who in turn allowed them to enforce religious law among the Jews.

Strategy Number 4—Supervise Piety: The Pharisees were the minority party in the Great Sanhedrin. They looked to bring about change through rigorous adherence to the law, including expanded laws that went well beyond the Scriptures. The Pharisees' relationship with Rome was uneasy compared with the Sadducees, and the Pharisees were more popular among the common people.

Strategy Number 5—Revolutionize: The Zealots were revolutionary Jews who wanted to violently overthrow Rome. They attempted a revolt in AD 66. It didn't work out, and like Babylon before them, the Roman army came to Jerusalem and completely destroyed the temple in AD 70.

Strategy Number 6—Hope in the Lord: Some Jews still believed God would send the Messiah to deliver humanity and initiate His kingdom. In Luke 2, Simeon and Anna recognize Jesus as the One who would be a light to the Gentiles and the redeemer of Jerusalem. This remnant didn't have political power, but they patiently trusted in God to keep His promises.

And Then There's Rome: Roman politics that had nothing to do with the Jews or Jerusalem also complicated the world in the time of Jesus. The Jews were often on the receiving end of fallout from high-stakes politics and court intrigue among Roman politicians jockeying for power.

The Fullness of Time: The New Testament says the perfect, God-ordained moment for Jesus to appear had come. Galatians 4:4 reads,

"But when the set time had fully come, God sent his Son, born of a woman, born under the law."

The New Testament Completes the Old Testament: The Old Testament sets up the problem and optimistically points to the solution. The New Testament tells the story of that promised solution. It completes the story arcs, prophecies, motifs, and themes of the Old Testament by telling the accounts of Jesus and the arrival of the Holy Spirit to lead the church, which is made up of people from all nations.

VITAL STATS

Position: 40 of 66.
Chapters: 28.
Verses: 1,071.
Word Count: 18,346 (16/66).
Most-Used Words: Jesus, kingdom, Son of Man, heaven, Father, Son, disciple, law.
Group: Gospels.
Audience: Jews.
Date: AD 50–70.
Popularity Rank: 2 of 66.

Lightning-Fast Summary: The Old Testament tells the story of a terrible curse of sin and death that afflicts all of humanity, but it also looks forward to a deliverer from God's chosen people who will break the curse and defeat death.

In Matthew, He shows up.

Unique Feature: Matthew is the connective tissue between the Old Testament and the New Testament.

This book makes it clear that the New Testament isn't a new religion, and Jesus isn't a new God. Rather, Jesus is the fulfillment of the Old Testament prophets and the completion of the Old Testament story. This isn't a new story; it's the next chapter in the story we've been following throughout the whole Bible.

What's a Gospel and Why Are There Four? If you're reading straight through the Bible, this is a new category of book for you. The term *gospel* literally means "good news," and the first four books of the New Testament (called the four gospels) all tell the story of Jesus as the Messiah who is predicted in the Old Testament. The first three (Matthew, Mark, and Luke) have a lot in common in terms of details, storytelling beats, and words from Jesus Himself. John is the last of the gospels, and he emphasizes different parts of Jesus' life and teachings. Each gospel writer brings a unique perspective to the story and complements one another.

Who Wrote It? Matthew (who also went by Levi). He was a Jew who collected taxes for the Romans. In Matthew 9:9, Jesus comes by his tax booth and says, "Follow me," and Matthew gets up and follows Him.

Matthew knows the Old Testament like the back of his hand. He's cognizant of the big stories and the subtle details, and he shares those on every page of his book.

Purpose: To convince Jews that Jesus is the Messiah and to help them understand Him and His kingdom.

Years Covered: Matthew opens with a genealogy that goes clear back to Abraham, but all of the action happens around Jesus' life. Jesus was probably born somewhere between 6 and 4 BC and died in the late 20s or very early 30s AD, so the book covers upwards of thirty-five years.

Lopsided Timeline: Only the first two chapters deal with Jesus' early life. The remaining twenty-six chapters cover the last three years of His life, when He was ministering in public.

Original Language: Greek (with a few Aramaic words and phrases).

Original Audience: Each of the gospel writers had a different audience in mind when they wrote (that's part of why there are four accounts of Jesus' life in the Bible). Matthew writes specifically to Jews who are trying to figure out if Jesus is the Messiah, the King who God promised would rule on David's throne forever.

Tone and Feel: Matthew exudes delight at how God has perfectly executed His ancient redemptive plan through Jesus. It's gritty, heady, and even violent in places, but overall the tone is joyful, because the hope that God promised for centuries has finally arrived in Jesus.

Where It Is Set: Most of the book happens in the rural northern region of Galilee, and the final act happens in Jerusalem.

Stuff You Can Still Physically Look At: Tons of stuff from Matthew remains. Jesus' home base of Capernaum, the site of the Sermon on the Mount, and the ruins of ancient Nazareth stand out.

Parts You Might Recognize Even If You Haven't Read the Bible: Jesus, Mary, the Magi (wise men), John the Baptist, Peter, the Golden Rule, "Blessed are the meek," Jesus walking on water, Pontius Pilate, the crucifixion, the resurrection.

Important Character: Jesus is the most important character in Matthew and the Bible as a whole.

Supporting Cast: The rest of the characters in Matthew all fit into one of three categories:

- Jesus' followers—They might not understand everything, but they trust Jesus and follow Him. As the book unfolds, they figure out He is the Messiah.
- Jesus' enemies—These are the religious leaders. They're threatened by Jesus and want Him gone.
- The squishy middle—Sometimes called the crowds; these people don't know what to make of Jesus, but they can't deny He's interesting.

The assumption of the book is that in the beginning, you'll identify with the squishy middle, but by the end, you'll see that Jesus is the Messiah.

How It's Built: The book of Matthew is constructed around five big speeches from Jesus.

The Dramatic Prologue: Matthew starts with a genealogy showing how Jesus is descended from Abraham, David, the captives in Babylon, and the rebuilders in Persia. Jesus is born in Bethlehem, the city of David, and King Herod tries to kill Him, so Joseph and Mary flee to Egypt, then return after Herod dies and live in Nazareth. Jesus' cousin John the Baptist leads a revival and baptizes Jesus, who is affirmed by God the Father and the Holy Spirit.

Jesus Passes the Test: The devil tempts Jesus in the wilderness, but unlike everyone before Him, Jesus passes the test. He's made of stronger stuff than all the other characters we've met so far. After forty days of resisting the devil, Jesus calls His first disciples and starts His public ministry.

Speech One—The Sermon on the Mount: Matthew 5–7 are three of the most theologically important chapters in the whole Bible. In them,

Jesus lays out the values of His kingdom, while saying that He hasn't come to abolish the Law but to fulfill it (5:17). Even the people who don't like Him have to admit He teaches with authority, and not like the teachers of the law (7:29). Over the rest of His ministry, Jesus demonstrates His authority over pretty much everything, including the law, ritual cleanliness, time, distance, disease, the forces of nature, and even death.

Speech Two—Mission: In Matthew 10, Jesus sends out His twelve disciples. They go to the Jewish people in Galilee and tell them that the promised kingdom is at hand. Somewhere in here, John the Baptist gets arrested by Herod and is eventually executed. The more the message of Jesus goes out, the more people follow Jesus, but also the more resistance Jesus gets from the Jewish religious leaders (especially the Pharisees).

Speech Three—Parables: The resistance to Jesus makes everyone wonder how this whole kingdom thing will play out, and in Matthew 13, Jesus speaks to those questions with a bunch of parables (stories illustrating theological truth). The opposition to Jesus intensifies, and He starts to direct His time toward intense mentoring of His disciples.

Important Interlude—The Son of God: In chapter 16, Jesus asks who His disciples believe He is, and finally Peter just comes out and says what's been obvious from the beginning: "You are the Messiah, the Son of the living God" (v. 16). Jesus affirms this and then tells His disciples that He's going to Jerusalem to get killed by the religious leadership, but also that He'll be raised back to life on the third day. Soon afterward, Peter, James, and John see Jesus in His heavenly glory talking with Moses and Elijah, and God says, "This is my Son, whom I love; with him I am well pleased. Listen to him!" (17:5).

Speech Four—The Church: In chapter 18, Jesus sets His followers up for success after He's gone by explaining what the church will look like. Then they make their way to Jerusalem, where Jesus receives a hero's welcome as He rides into town on a donkey, fulfilling Zechariah 9:9. The religious leaders throw everything they have at Him, trying to embarrass Him publicly, but

Jesus is too smart and too right, and the religious leaders end up looking like fools. Eventually, they decide that if they can't discredit Him, they'll just have to kill Him, and they get to work on a plan.

Speech Five—The Future: In Matthew 24–25, Jesus tells His disciples how things will play out in the future. He tells them to live as though He might return in glory at any moment, but also to pace themselves in service of the kingdom for the long haul. Jesus eats with them one last time, and there He initiates the Lord's Supper, saying that His body will be given and His blood will be shed for the forgiveness of sins. After that, Jesus is arrested by the religious leaders under cover of darkness, convicted in a farce of a trial, and handed over to Pontius Pilate to be sentenced to death.

The Curse Defeated: A Roman execution squad crucifies Jesus. They verify that He's dead, and a follower buries Him in a tomb guarded by Roman soldiers. Three days later, He's raised and meets back up with His disciples in physical, human form. He commissions them to go to the whole world—to all the nations, not just the Jews—and to make disciples of everyone, teaching them everything He commanded and baptizing them in the name of the Father, the Son, and the Holy Spirit (28:19–20).

Did That Seem like a Lot? Well, there's a ton more in Matthew. It's a dense, action-packed book, with huge chunks dedicated to the teaching of Jesus. Like the other gospels, this book describes the central moment in God's redemptive plan.

Theme: Jesus is the Messiah, promised throughout the Old Testament. He is the King who will reign on the throne of David forever. He is the Son of God who died to forgive the sins of all mankind and to break the curse from back in Eden. The person who has eyes to see should recognize this, repent of their sin, and follow Jesus.

Key Verses: Peter's confession of Christ in Matthew 16:16 (quoted earlier), and also Matthew 5:17—"Do not think that I have come to abolish the Law or the Prophets; I have not come to abolish them but to fulfill them."

If You Don't Have Time to Read the Whole Thing, at Least Read: The Sermon on the Mount in Matthew 5–7.

When You Visualize Matthew, Picture: A crown.

VITAL STATS

Position: 41 of 66.
Chapters: 16.
Verses: 678.
Word Count: 11,304 (23/66).
Most-Used Words: Jesus, man, disciples, people, crowd.
Group: Gospels.
Audience: Romans.
Date: AD 50–68.
Popularity Rank: 13 of 66.

MARK

Lightning-Fast Summary : A rapid-fire, action-heavy account of the life, death, and resurrection of Jesus meant to show that He is the Son of God.

Unique Feature: Mark is full of specific, vivid details that probably came from Peter. Reliable tradition says Mark traveled with Peter and used his sermons and stories as a source.

Who Wrote It? Mark (who goes by John Mark in the Bible). All the gospels are technically anonymous, but early Christians pointed only to Mark as the author of this book. When Mark was young, he traveled with the apostle Paul (a very important Christian leader from later in the New Testament who traveled the Roman world establishing churches). Mark went on Paul's first missionary journey but tapped out in the early going, so Paul didn't take him on any more trips. Instead, as Mark matured, he traveled with Barnabas and eventually Peter.

Purpose: To convince Romans (or anyone who might read it) that Jesus is the Son of God and the Servant-Messiah predicted in the Old Testament.

Years Covered: Mark doesn't talk about Jesus' birth. Instead, he starts with the ministry of John the Baptist and then follows the story through to Jesus' death and resurrection. The whole story covers only a few years leading up to Jesus' crucifixion around AD 30.

Original Language: Greek (with a few Aramaic words and phrases).

Type of Book: Persuasive theological narrative.

Original Audience: Mostly Romans.

Mark's Not Shy: This book explodes out of the gate with its thesis in the opening line: "The beginning of the good news about Jesus the Messiah, the Son of God" (1:1). In one brief declaration, he tells you Jesus is the promised deliverer, that there is only one God and Jesus is His Son (an idea that would have piqued the curiosity of a Roman reader). Also, implied by the fact that you're reading it, this good news is for *you,* no matter who you are or where you're from.

At the time, most readers knew dang well that Rome executed Jesus. The opening line has Mark saying they got it wrong.

Tone and Feel: Mark is always pushing the action forward. He constantly uses the phrase *at once* (or *immediately*) to keep the story hurrying forward. Jesus is presented as a man of action who knows exactly who He is and what He's here to do. Among the Gospels, Mark records the fewest words of Jesus. He emphasizes Jesus' deeds. A presentation like that would resonate with a first-century audience in Rome.

But Mark also focuses on Jesus' humble service toward people from all walks of life, people who rank way beneath the Son of God. That would have made a Roman reader's compass spin.

No Prerequisites Required: Mark doesn't assume his audience knows the ins and outs of Jewish culture, politics, and religion. When that kind of stuff is necessary for Mark's story to make sense, he takes a moment to explain it (like in 7:3–4, where he quickly describes a few Jewish purification rituals).

Important Characters: Jesus (who is the most important character in the Bible), Peter, James, John, John the Baptist, Caiaphas the high priest, Judas, and Mary Magdalene.

How It's Built and Where the Stories Happen: The first half stacks story upon story of Jesus doing amazing things that, when considered as a whole, make it clear He's the Messiah, the Son of God. (Peter finally says in Mark 8:29 what we've all been thinking: "You are the Messiah.") This stuff mostly happens in rural Galilee, north of Judea. In the second half, the action moves south, toward Jerusalem, where Jesus is crucified and raised back to life.

Mark Likes Isaiah: Mark doesn't reference the Old Testament much, but he knew how much Romans liked soothsaying and prophecy, so when he does go there, he's keen on quoting the great prophet Isaiah to show that, unlike gods and sons of gods in Roman myths that triumph with pride and physical prowess, the true Son of God was always predicted to triumph through humility and suffering.

Unsung Hero: The Roman centurion who led the execution squad that killed Jesus. After it's all done, he reflects on what he had just seen and makes a confession about Christ that echoes Peter's when he says, "Surely this man was the Son of God!" (15:39). It's an admission of both Jesus' deity and innocence, and it would have been particularly powerful for a Roman reader. When you come to the end of the book, the story is suddenly over, and you're left to make sense of what you've just seen. It seems like Mark is hoping that the centurion's conversion (or "come to Jesus" moment) will inspire your own.

Villain: The religious leaders and Roman authorities who wrongly convict and kill the Son of God.

Most Shocking Moment: When God allows His Son to be put to death by corrupt people to save corrupt people.

How Should I Feel? Compelled by the nature and character of Jesus, the Son of God, and moved by His suffering to give you forgiveness of your sins.

Theme: Jesus is the Servant-Messiah and the Son of God. When Peter figured it out, he followed Him, but when the religious leaders figured it out, they rejected Him. What will you do?

Key Verse: Mark 1:1—"The beginning of the good news about Jesus the Messiah, the Son of God."

If You Don't Have Time to Read the Whole Thing, at Least Read: Mark 10:35–45, where Jesus shows Himself to be the suffering servant Messiah.

Bonus Reading: Go back to the Old Testament and read the four servant songs of Isaiah that predict who Jesus will be and what He'll come to do. They can be found in Isaiah 42:1–9; 49:1–13; 50:4–11; and 52:13–53:12.

When You Visualize Mark, Picture: The cross.

Mount of Olives, Jerusalem.

VITAL STATS

Position: 42 of 66.
Chapters: 24.
Verses: 1,151.
Word Count: 19,482 (12/66).
Most-Used Words: God, Lord, Jesus, Spirit, man, kingdom, heaven, disciples.
Group: Gospels.
Audience: Literally everyone.
Date: AD 50–68.
Popularity Rank: 4 of 66.

LUKE

Lightning-Fast Summary: Jesus is the compassionate Savior of the world; He's for everyone.

Unique Feature: Luke has a sequel called Acts, but it's not the next book of the Bible. The gospel of John sits between the two parts written by Luke.

Who Wrote It? Luke. He was a physician and a good friend to Paul who traveled along on some of the missionary journeys described in the book of Acts. Luke is the only Gentile to write a book of the Bible, and he's the biggest contributor to the New Testament (by total word count).

How He Wrote It: Matthew and John were disciples, so they wrote about events they saw with their own eyes. Mark most likely partnered with Peter, who was there for all of it as well. But Luke probably never met Jesus and was a part of the second generation of Christians. He knew people would wonder where he got his information, so he opens his book by explaining that he did research and talked to eyewitnesses so he could give an "orderly account" (1:1–3).

The Rich Guy Who Probably Funded Luke's Work: Luke says he's done all the work to write this account for someone named Most Excellent Theophilus. This title indicates that Theophilus was someone with enough wealth and influence to commission a project of this scale. He gets mentioned at the beginning of Acts as well, but his exact identity is a mystery.

Purpose: To give an ordered, reliable, carefully researched account of Jesus' life and teachings. Luke wants people from all walks of life to see that Jesus is the Savior of the world, and he wants them to be confident it's true.

Rome Was Wrong: Understandably, Luke is writing to a wide audience around the Roman world, and they would wonder why Jesus got rejected by His own people and executed by Rome. Luke makes it clear that Jesus was unjustly convicted, and that His conviction and death were God's plan from the beginning.

Time Covered: Around thirty-five years, from a bit before Jesus' birth to forty days after Jesus' resurrection. Luke starts in roughly 5 BC and wraps up in the ballpark of AD 30.

Original Language: Greek (with a few Aramaic words and phrases).

Type of Book: Persuasive theological narrative.

Tone and Feel: Luke is brave, outside-the-box, and wildly optimistic. Luke's tone mirrors Jesus' demeanor—bad things happen, but Jesus resolutely sets His face toward redemption and powers through all resistance.

Important Characters: Jesus, Mary (His mother), John the Baptist and his parents, the disciples (especially Peter, James, and John), a group of faithful women (especially Mary Magdalane), Judas (who betrays Jesus), the Pharisees and Sadducees (religious leaders who opposed Jesus), and the Roman governor Pontius Pilate (who sends Jesus to the cross).

Christmas Prologue: Luke is where we get most of the details of the Christmas story. The gospel opens with a grand prologue about the birth of Jesus. The angel Gabriel appears to Mary, who is a virgin, and tells her she's going to be with child through the Holy Spirit. Joseph, her betrothed, supports and protects her, and the baby is born in a manger in Bethlehem (the city of David). The story ends with Luke 2:52: "And Jesus grew in wisdom and stature, and in favor with God and man."

Jesus Is for Everyone: In chapters 3–9, Jesus is mostly in rural Galilee. He's baptized by John the Baptist, tempted by the devil, and followed by His disciples. During this time, He teaches about the kingdom of God and specifically shows care and attention to people on the fringes, like a sinful woman, the diseased, the poor, tax collectors, and even Gentiles. His teaching, His miracles, and the company He keeps make it clear that the kingdom of God is for everyone, just as the Old Testament prophets envisioned.

Pivot Point: Not everyone is excited about this. By Luke 6, "the Pharisees and the teachers of the law were furious and began to discuss with one another what they might do to Jesus" (v. 11). Jesus knows they're going to kill Him (it was the plan all along), and in Luke 9:51, the whole story pivots as Jesus resolutely sets out for Jerusalem (even though it's the stronghold of those who want Him dead). He travels slowly, performing miracles, gathering crowds, and teaching famous parables like those of the good Samaritan and the prodigal son.

Final Act: In Luke 19, the common people welcome Jesus into Jerusalem, shouting, "Blessed is the king who comes in the name of the Lord!" (v. 38). That gets the religious leaders even more agitated. They have Jesus arrested, and hand Him over to Pontius Pilate for sentencing. Pilate doesn't see a reason to move forward, but to appease the crowds, he sends Jesus to the cross. Jesus dies, is buried, and is resurrected on the third day.

After the resurrection, Jesus explains to His disciples how the whole Old Testament points to Him. Then He tells them to wait in Jerusalem until He sends them the Holy Spirit, and with that, Jesus physically ascends into heaven, and that's the end of the book.

Unsung Hero: She's not unsung at all but still deserves to be mentioned here. It's Mary, Jesus' mother. She demonstrated amazing faith in hard circumstances and believed God. She composed the Magnificat—one of the most profound songs of praise ever written (1:46–55).

Most Shocking Moment: When Jesus publicly reads stuff about the Messiah from Isaiah at a synagogue, and then says, "Today this scripture is fulfilled in your hearing." The other people in the synagogue are so mad that they try to throw Him off a cliff, but He's able to pass through them and be on His way (4:18–30).

Theme: Jesus is the compassionate Savior of the whole world, and no matter who you are or where you're from, you should trust in Him.

Key Verse: Luke 19:10—"For the Son of Man came to seek and to save the lost."

If You Don't Have Time to Read the Whole Thing, at Least Read: The parable of the lost son in Luke 15 and the story of the resurrection in Luke 24.

When You Visualize Luke, Picture: The nativity scene.

Synagogue ruins, Capernaum.
malajscy/stock.adobe.com

VITAL STATS

Position: 43 of 66.
Chapters: 21.
Verses: 879.
Word Count: 15,635 (20/66).
Most-Used Words: Father, Son, believe, world, life, light, love.
Group: Gospels.
Audience: Christians everywhere, and all people considering Jesus.
Date: AD 70–100.
Popularity Rank: 3 of 66.

Lightning-Fast Summary: The story of the teachings, works, death, and resurrection of Jesus that together show that Jesus is the Messiah, the Son of God, and God in the flesh.

Unique Feature: The first three gospels (Matthew, Mark, and Luke) are called "the Synoptics." That means "with the same eye" because these narratives have so much perspective in common and cover so many of the same details. John's style is different from that of the Synoptics, and most of all, he stresses more than the others that Jesus is God in the flesh.

90 Percent: That's how much of the stuff in John is unique to John among the four gospels.

Who Wrote It? John, the disciple whom Jesus loved. John is believed to be the only one of the original twelve disciples who wasn't martyred but lived to an old age. He also wrote 1, 2, and 3 John and the book of Revelation.

The Latest Gospel: Most people think John wrote his gospel last. In the same way you can sort of tell if something was written in the 1950s or the 1990s, some scholars are able to catch a bunch of little hints that John wrote near the end of the first century AD. Early church leaders say John wrote after the Synoptics were already circulating widely because he wanted to supplement them.

Purpose: John could not be more explicit about why he wrote what he wrote and what he wants you to get out of it. In John 20:30–31, he spells it out: "Jesus performed many other signs in the presence of his disciples, which are not recorded in this book. But these are written *that you may believe that Jesus is the Messiah, the Son of God, and that by believing you may have life in his name*" (emphasis added).

Time Covered: Around thirty-five years; from a bit before Jesus' birth to forty days after Jesus' resurrection. John starts in roughly 5 BC and wraps up around AD 30.

Original Language: Greek (with a few Aramaic words and phrases).

Type of Book: Persuasive theological narrative.

Tone and Feel: The author is convinced that the Jesus thing is the most important truth of anything ever, and he wants to convince you, but he knows it's a lot to take in, so he writes with patience and empathy toward the reader, opening with a huge claim and then layering on detail upon detail until you see it too.

Important Characters: Mary (Jesus' mother), John the Baptist and his parents, the disciples (especially Peter, James, and John), a group of faithful women (especially Mary Magdalene), Judas (who betrays Jesus), the Pharisees and Sadducees (religious leaders who opposed Jesus), and the Roman governor Pontius Pilate (who sends Jesus to the cross).

The Boldest First Sentence of Any Book Ever: "In the beginning was the Word, and the Word was with God, and the Word was God."

In the beginning of John, there's no genealogy (as in Matthew), Old Testament quote from Isaiah (as in the Synoptics), or beautiful birth prologue (as in Luke). Nope, none of that. Instead, opening with the same phrase as Genesis opens, John goes even further back, before time as we know it began, when there was only God and nothing had yet been made. And then he says that Jesus was not only there, and always has been there, but that Jesus is God.

What John Means When He Calls Jesus "the Word": *Word,* used throughout John 1, refers to Jesus. In Greek, it's *logos,* a word used to express the underlying rational order that makes existence work. The context of chapter 1 and the rest of John makes it ultra-obvious that when John says *logos* (Word), he's talking about Jesus, and presenting Him as God in the flesh.

John Is Saying That Jesus Is God: John 1 presents the *logos* (Jesus) as being God and also as being with God from eternity. Then in chapters 14 and 16, Jesus talks about the Holy Spirit. All that to say, John presents God as the Trinity—one God, eternally existent in three persons who are distinct from one another. Jesus is the Son of God, and Jesus is God.

You Can't Just Say Stuff Like That: If you make claims this bold, you have to defend them, and that's what John is about. The rest of the book is built around a series of seven big miraculous signs that point to Jesus' true identity, and seven "I am" statements Jesus makes that identify Him as God, using the ancient name that God revealed to Moses at the burning bush in Exodus 3:14—Yahweh, which means I AM WHO I AM.

The Same but Different: The big picture of John's story looks like Matthew, Mark, and Luke: Jesus' teachings and miracles convince many to follow Him, but they anger the religious leaders, who eventually convince Rome to execute Jesus, who then on the third day is raised from the dead.

That said, John includes several stories that don't come up in the other gospels: Jesus turning water into wine at a wedding, meeting in secret with Nicodemus the Pharisee, talking with a Samaritan woman by a well, raising his friend Lazarus from the dead, and washing His disciples' feet.

Salvation: When John the Baptist sees Jesus approaching him, he says, "Look, the Lamb of God, who takes away the sin of the world!" (1:29). Jesus is the curse-breaker.

Theme: Jesus is the Messiah, the Word, the Son of God, and God. Anyone who believes in Him will have eternal life.

Most Shocking Moment: In John 4, when Jesus talks alone with a Samaritan woman at a well. This conversation sets a pattern of Jesus (and the church) welcoming and including women and ethnic outsiders, which was unthinkable to many at the time.

It also shows Jesus quickly resolving an ancient ethnic controversy between the Samaritans and Jews by saying that He is the living water for everyone.

Most Famous Verse: John 3:16—"For God so loved the world that he gave his one and only Son, that whoever believes in him shall not perish but have eternal life."

Key Verses: John 1:1; 3:16; 20:31 (all quoted previously); and 14:6 where Jesus makes one of His seven "I am" statements: "I am the way and the truth and the life. No one comes to the Father except through me."

If You Don't Have Time to Read the Whole Thing, at Least Read: The seven "I am" statements in John 6:35; 8:12; 10:7–14; 11:25; 14:6; and 15:1–17.

When You Visualize John, Picture: "I AM."

Jacob's Well, Nablus.

holylandphotos.com

VITAL STATS

Position: 44 of 66.
Chapters: 28.
Verses: 1,007.
Word Count: 18,450 (15/66).
Most-Used Words: God, Lord, Jesus, apostles, Peter, Paul, believe, synagogue.
Group: History of the early church.
Audience: Christians everywhere.
Date: AD 62 or a little after.
Popularity Rank: 10 of 66.

ACTS

Lightning-Fast Summary: Jesus ascends into heaven, and the disciples take the message of Jesus to the world with the help of the Holy Spirit and new generations of Jewish and Gentile Christians.

Unique Feature: Acts is a sequel to the gospel of Luke. It picks up immediately where Luke left off (there's even a little bit of overlap to get the reader back up to speed), and it's the only book outside of the Gospels that has the incarnate Jesus in it as an on-screen character.

Who Wrote It? Luke, the same guy who wrote the gospel of Luke. He was a physician, friend, and traveling partner with the apostle Paul. He is the greatest contributor to the New Testament by total word count.

Commissioned: It's likely that someone named Theophilus commissioned both Luke and Acts. Luke addresses both books to him and says he set out to put together an orderly account of all that happened with Jesus (and since).

Luke Wasn't in Luke, but He Is in Acts: Luke wasn't around for the life of Jesus, but he says he consulted lots of people who were (Luke 1:1–4). Luke wasn't there for the beginning of Acts either, but eventually he joins up with Paul in the city of Troas (Acts 16:11). Up to that point in Acts, Luke uses third-person pronouns to narrate the action, but after Troas, there are several big chunks of Acts where Luke uses first-person plural pronouns (we/us/our) to describe the parts of the story he was a part of.

The "we" passages are fun to read because it feels more like you're along for the ride with Paul and Luke.

Purpose: At the most basic level, Acts is the next part of the story, covering what happens after Jesus. On a deeper level, Acts shows how the Holy Spirit (who is God) is in charge of opening people's eyes and ears to the message of Jesus and building the church from all the nations, just as the Old Testament predicted.

Acts Answers a Question: How did Christianity happen? How did it go from a few people huddled in a room in Jerusalem after their leader got executed to literally the biggest, most important movement in the history of everything?

Time Covered: Acts only gives us the first thirty-five-ish years of that answer, but it explains the foundational factors that caused Christianity to explode beyond its initial Jewish borders and set in motion the events that would take the message of Jesus to every corner of the planet.

When Did It Happen? Acts starts a few weeks after Jesus' crucifixion (in the late 20s or early 30s AD) and wraps up around AD 62, when Paul is under house arrest in Rome during the reign of Emperor Nero.

Stuff You Can Still Physically Look At: So much! You can visit the ruins of almost every city mentioned in Acts, and some (like Ephesus) are super well-preserved. Many have inscriptions and monuments that confirm historical details in Acts.

Original Language: Greek (with a few Aramaic words and phrases).

Type of Book: True history in a classical Greco-Roman style.

Tone and Feel: Intrepid. All kinds of problems and resistance keep happening, but Jesus' followers take the beatings and keep going, undaunted.

Important Characters: Jesus always gets first billing, even if He's only in the book for a minute. Peter plays a huge role in the first half, and then the story leaves him behind to follow Paul and his friends, who include Barnabas, John Mark (who wrote Mark), Silas, Timothy, and Luke himself. Stephen, Philip, Gamaliel,

Simon the sorcerer, and Roman governors Felix and Festus also play important parts.

Two Verses to Lay Out the Plot: The risen Jesus is still with the disciples when the book begins, and they all seem to think it might be time for some sort of Old Testament–style judgment against the institutions that killed Him, but Jesus has something very different in mind: "It is not for you to know the times or dates the Father has set by his own authority. But you will receive power when the Holy Spirit comes on you; and you will be my witnesses in Jerusalem, and in all Judea and Samaria, and to the ends of the earth" (1:7–8).

The rest of the book of Acts uses those verses as an outline. First, the disciples preach the message of Jesus in Jerusalem (chapters 1–6), then they take it to historic Judea and Samaria (chapters 6–12), and finally the message spreads all over the Roman Empire (chapters 12–28).

Jerusalem—The First Revival: Shortly after Jesus ascends into heaven, the Holy Spirit (who is God) arrives in Jerusalem in miraculous and dramatic fashion. Something that looks like tongues of fire appears over the heads of the disciples, and suddenly all the foreigners there can hear the disciples in their own native languages. Peter quotes the prophet Joel and explains that Jesus is the Messiah. The diverse crowd is moved, and three thousand people become Christians on that day.

The Holy Spirit keeps doing miracles, masses of people follow Jesus, and the religious leaders get mad. They flog the apostles and tell them to stop talking about Jesus, but Peter and the others count it a blessing and keep preaching. The church grows fast, and a second generation of leaders steps up to meet needs. One of them, named Stephen, runs afoul of the religious leaders, and they stone him to death, which pushes the disciples to take the message to Judea and Samaria.

Judea and Samaria: Saul, one of the leaders at Stephen's stoning, decides to pursue and punish the Christians as they scatter to Judea and Samaria, but while Saul is traveling, he has a miraculous encounter with Jesus and switches sides. Saul starts being called Paul and wins the trust of the Christians he used to persecute.

Late 1800s photo of Straight Street, Damascus.

Public domain

Meanwhile, God tells Peter that all the food that had been unclean in the Old Testament is now clean. Immediately after that, the Holy Spirit arranges a meeting between Peter and a Roman centurion that ends with this powerful man and his whole Gentile family becoming Christians and experiencing miracles just like the Jewish disciples had.

The Ends of the Earth: From chapter 12 until the end of the book, the focus shifts to Paul (who really is the main human character of Acts). Paul takes three huge trips around the Mediterranean Sea, Asia Minor (modern-day Turkey), and Greece. On these trips, he takes massive physical abuse (his attackers thought he was dead once and dragged his body out of town). Still, he preaches Jesus fearlessly and establishes Christian communities all over the Roman world. When Paul takes the message back to Jerusalem, he's arrested and transferred to Rome on a harrowing journey. The book ends with him under house arrest in Rome, but he's allowed to write letters and preach the message of Jesus.

Babel Undone: Back in Genesis 11, God scrambled human language at the Tower of Babel, and in the book of Acts, He puts it back together through the language miracle at Pentecost and by making a new family of faith in Jesus that transcends all social, ethnic, cultural, and linguistic barriers.

Theme: God will build His church by His power, and it will reach all people to the ends of the earth.

Key Verses: Acts 1:8 (quoted earlier) and Acts 2:38, where Peter says, "Repent and be baptized, every one of you, in the name of Jesus Christ for the forgiveness of your sins. And you will receive the gift of the Holy Spirit."

If You Don't Have Time to Read the Whole Thing, at Least Read: Acts 2, 7, and 9.

When You Visualize Acts, Picture: Tongues of fire.

VITAL STATS

Position: 45 of 66.
Chapters: 16.
Verses: 433.
Word Count: 7,111 (28/66).
Most-Used Words: God, law, faith, sin, justified, righteousness, Christ, grace, flesh, spirit, Israel.
Group: Letters to churches.
Audience: Christians in Rome.
Written From: Corinth.
Date: AD 57.
Popularity Rank: 8 of 66.

Lightning-Fast Summary: A letter from Paul to Roman Christians that explains God's righteousness and human unrighteousness, and how God gives His righteousness to Jews and Gentiles alike through Jesus.

Unique Feature: Romans dives deeper into the mechanics of salvation than any other book of the Bible.

Who Wrote It? The apostle Paul, a guy for whom salvation was not an academic abstraction. He used to persecute Christians but then was transformed when Jesus confronted him on the road to Damascus in Acts 9.

Original Language: Paul wrote Romans, and all his letters, in Greek. It was the perfect language for Paul's purposes because Jews and Gentiles spoke it, and it was sufficiently sophisticated to carry important theological ideas.

Letters Until Revelation: From here until the final book of the Bible, it's all letters passed around among early Christians. These next twenty-one books feel much different from the Gospels and Acts, which are narratives, but these letters still have tension, stories, and stakes. The first nine letters (including Romans) are from Paul to specific churches somewhere around the empire. The next four are letters from Paul to other Christian leaders he's helping (these are called the "Pastoral Epistles"). The final six letters are by James, John, Peter, and Jude (plus whoever wrote Hebrews). They're written to Christians in general and are sometimes called the "General Epistles."

What Prompted Romans? It's AD 57, and Paul is facing a tough decision. He's halfway between Rome and Jerusalem in the city of Corinth. It's his third missionary journey, and on the one hand, he wants to keep going west to visit the young Christian community in Rome (the most influential city in the world). He's heard about a tension in the church there between Jewish and Gentile Christians, and he's also got ambitions to take the gospel from Rome on to Spain. But on the other hand, Paul is carrying around a bunch of money given to him by Gentile Christians to help their Jewish brothers and sisters in Jerusalem during a horrible famine. The collection is more than timely cash; it represents a huge moment in building the unity of the multiethnic global church. Ultimately, Paul decides he has to deliver the money immediately and in person, even if it means that Rome and Spain must wait.

For now, a letter will have to do.

Purpose: If Paul couldn't visit personally, he at least wanted to shore up the Roman Christians' understanding of God's redemptive work. In the past, Paul had seen outside agitators sneak into fledgling Gentile churches to sow confusion about how a person is forgiven and made right with God. He wanted to prevent that from happening again, and he wanted to bolster the Romans' clarity and confidence in the gospel so they could thrive in it themselves and be better equipped to reach others with it. Paul wants them to be locked in on the theology of salvation in Christ.

Tone and Feel: Theologically complex but clearly and practically explained.

To What Do I Owe the Pleasure? These are letters, so they all start with some sort of personal hello, with a few words about the occasion of the letter included. After that, there's often a ten-thousand-foot view statement of basic Christian theology in the form of a blessing.

Appian Way, a Roman road.

Francisco Javier Diaz/Shutterstock.com

Most of Paul's letters also include a list of personal greetings at the very end. Romans has all these elements.

The Good News: Throughout the body of the letter, Paul uses plain language to lay out a handful of related theological truths that add up to a clear picture of what salvation is and how it works. Paul explains that God alone is righteous, and that people aren't (3:23). That's a problem because the wages of sin is death (6:23). So we're doomed unless God steps in and finds a way to pay the costs of sin and give us His righteousness. Paul shares in Romans 5 the good news is that God has done exactly that. Those who put their faith in Jesus have forgiveness for sin, are justified and given right standing before God, are spared the penalty of their sin, and have peace with God. Paul makes it clear that this isn't a new revelation, but that salvation has always been by faith, citing in Romans 4 the example of Abraham. But salvation from sin isn't the endgame. Paul goes on to explain in Romans 8 how the Holy Spirit works in Christians to defeat sin and nurture lives of obedience toward God.

Theme: God is righteous in everything, including His dealings with Israel and all humanity. Salvation happens when God's righteousness is given to unrighteous Jews and Gentiles alike through faith in Jesus.

If You Don't Have Time to Read the Whole Thing, at Least Read: If a person only reads one New Testament letter, Romans is the way to go, but if time doesn't allow you to read the whole thing, there's a lot to be gleaned from this classic list of verses: Romans 1:16–17; 3:10–18, 23; 5:1, 8; 6:23; 8:1, 38–39; 10:9, 13.

When You Visualize Romans, Picture: A well-marked path leading to the cross.

VITAL STATS

Position: 46 of 66.
Chapters: 16.
Verses: 437.
Word Count: 6,830 (29/66).
Most-Used Words: God, Lord, Christ, body, spirit, love, church, law.
Group: Letters to churches.
Audience: Christians in Corinth.
Written From: Ephesus.
Date: AD 55.
Popularity Rank: 9 of 66.

1 CORINTHIANS

Lightning-Fast Summary: Paul writes to the church at Corinth, his most difficult church, to challenge them on issues of morality, internal strife, and prideful, chaotic worship.

Unique Feature: This is the first hard book of the New Testament. The Gospels tell the best story ever, and they all end with Jesus' glorious victory over sin and death. Acts recounts how the Holy Spirit relentlessly advances the good news to the whole world, and Romans is full of optimistic theology, explaining and celebrating the righteousness of God imparted to sinners. But 1 Corinthians is written to a church struggling with tons of issues. The Christians in Corinth have tasted the salvation described in Romans, but not the life of obedience in the Holy Spirit described in Romans.

Who Wrote It? Paul, who has tons of history with Corinth.

Original Language: All Greek.

Historical Setting: Corinth was a significant city-state in classical Greece that eventually got wiped out by the Romans in 146 BC. But a hundred years later, Julius Caesar resurrected Corinth as a built-from-scratch Roman colony because of its strategic location on a narrow pinch point of land between two huge chunks of Greece. Roman Corinth had two fully functioning harbors that served two completely separate seas, so if you think about what kind of shenanigans go on in a town with sailors coming in and out of a harbor and then double it, you've got a sense of how wild things were in Corinth. Corinth was synonymous with lewd sex stuff. Her patron goddess was Aphrodite, and the temple there was a notorious place for elaborate acts of immorality.

A Challenge or an Opportunity? Sure, Corinth being Corinthian presented a challenge for the church there, but it was also an opportunity for Christians to demonstrate the power of God over the allure of temptation to outsiders who sailed into Corinth from all over the world.

Paul's History with Corinth: Paul helped start the Corinthian church around AD 50, and he worked there for eighteen months (Acts 18:11). Paul moved on, and somewhere over the next five years, he heard about sexual immorality in the Corinthian church and wrote them a letter of correction (referenced in 1 Corinthians 5:9). That letter (lost to history) didn't solve things, but it did prompt the church in Corinth to write back to Paul with some follow-up questions, so Paul answered them with what we call 1 Corinthians, which he wrote from Ephesus during his third missionary journey around AD 55.

Why This Letter? Paul is writing because it was strategically vital to the spread of the gospel for this church to succeed, but more so, he's writing because he cares about these people and is heartbroken over the painful mess they find themselves in because of their sin, pride, and bad theology.

Tone and Feel: Firmly corrective but fatherly and pastoral. Paul's disappointment comes through but also his care.

Don't Act like Corinthians: For a corrective letter, 1 Corinthians opens quite tenderly, with an appeal to Christian unity through the example of Christ. Beginning in 1:20 and running through the end of chapter 6, Paul gets into the specifics of what they're getting wrong. He talks about their disunity, their lax sexual ethics, and their inability to deal with the messes as a church.

He calls them out for taking their church family disputes before secular magistrates. The heart of his accusation is that they're taking their cues from Corinthian culture instead of from Christ.

Now I'll Speak to Your Questions: In chapters 7–14, Paul speaks to family life and disorderly worship, and he also addresses a matter of conscience regarding eating perfectly good meat that had been sacrificed to an idol.

Be Assured: Finally, in chapters 15–16, Paul closes out his letter by reinforcing the witnessed, certain fact of Jesus' resurrection and appealing to the believers to stand firm because their work isn't in vain. In his closing remarks, he tells them how to take up money to help the Jewish Christians who are suffering from famine in Judea and extends lots of personal greetings.

Famous Body Metaphor: In chapter 12, Paul invites the Corinthians to think of the body counterculturally by comparing the church to a body with lots of parts that all do different things. He reminds them that they all need each other to be functional, whole, and effective.

Most Famous Passage You Might Recognize Even If You Haven't Read the Bible: First Corinthians 13, which beautifully describes mature, Christlike love. It's read at a lot of marriage ceremonies, and if you're a married Christian with a cross-stitching aunt, you probably got a sampler with this passage on it as a wedding gift.

Most Applicable Verse for Modern Audiences: 1 Corinthians 10:31—"So whether you eat or drink or whatever you do, do it all for the glory of God."

Theme Verse: 1 Corinthians 1:10—"I appeal to you, brothers and sisters, in the name of our Lord Jesus Christ, that all of you agree with one another in what you say and that there be no divisions among you, but that you be perfectly united in mind and thought."

Theme: Set aside pride to pursue holiness and be united in Christ.

If You Don't Have Time to Read the Whole Thing, at Least Read: 1 Corinthians 1 and 15.

When You Visualize 1 Corinthians, Picture: The body of Christ.

VITAL STATS

Position: 47 of 66.
Chapters: 13.
Verses: 257.
Word Count: 4,477 (35/66).
Most-Used Words: God, Christ, Lord, ministry, glory, grace, comfort.
Group: Letters to churches.
Audience: Christians in Corinth.
Written From: Macedonia.
Date: Late AD 55 or 56.
Popularity Rank: 17 of 66.

2 CORINTHIANS

Lightning-Fast Summary: Paul takes another run at trying to correct the ugliness in the church in Corinth.

Unique Feature: Second Corinthians may have the most 100-percent, verifiable, no-questions-asked certainty of authorship of anything in the Bible. Not only does the book have Paul's signature and sound exactly like Paul, but it's also chock-full of details from his life. The authorship of some books has been debated over the centuries, but no one has ever credibly challenged Paul's authorship of 2 Corinthians.

Who Wrote It? So, Paul.

Original Language: Paul wrote all his letters in Greek.

Tone and Feel: Second Corinthians feels like the moment you relax your defenses after you get into a heated argument with someone you care about.

Historical Setting: Corinth was a tough town known for having the loosest of morals.

Paul's History with Corinth, Part II: Paul helped start the church in Corinth, moved on, heard they were struggling, then wrote them letters to help (including 1 Corinthians). That didn't work, so Paul sneaked in a quick visit, which went poorly. Someone challenged Paul's authority, and

Paul quickly chased that bad visit with another letter, which has since been lost. While still on his third missionary journey a few months later, Paul found out that his letter had mostly softened the Corinthians' hearts. He was overjoyed and wrote them a follow-up letter, which we call 2 Corinthians.

Patching It Up: Things had gotten ugly in Corinth, and Paul had to say hard things to them to fix it. Now that things have simmered down, Paul is eager to build them back up. In the first nine chapters, Paul turns over his cards and explains his decision-making and reasons for not visiting sooner or longer. He also works through the question of the guy who challenged Paul's authority during Paul's last visit. Paul follows up on the gift he's gathering for the Jewish Christians who are suffering in Jerusalem and tells the Corinthians he's sending Titus to check in and collect it. This section pulls back the curtain on Paul's personality, planning, and priorities. Despite all the logistical and relationship stuff, it's still very theological (with a focus on the Holy Spirit), and it's very human.

Stuff's Mostly Good, but There Are Still Issues: In the final chapters, Paul speaks to the handful of Corinthian Christians who are still angry and are undermining him and the gospel. Jewish Christians from Judea had visited Corinth to preach a different message and to discredit Paul. Paul defends the legitimacy of his apostleship and authority from Jesus and calls out the Judean agitators, as well as the Corinthians who were going along with them.

How Did It Work Out in Corinth? Paul visited Corinth for the third time a year or so after he sent 2 Corinthians. There are hints that the visit went well, and he composed Romans while he was there. Things were good in Corinth for the next forty years, until Clement of Rome wrote an extrabiblical letter to them because they were again dealing with strife and disunity.

The church Paul founded thrived for several more centuries but went through cycles of floundering and recovery from about AD 400 through the Crusades as the city suffered from earthquakes, economic downturns, and invasion. Despite all that happened, Corinth has been continuously inhabited by Christians since Paul, and it is still there to this day.

So I guess the letters worked.

Ultra-Important Theology Verse About Jesus: 2 Corinthians 5:21—"God made him who had no sin to be sin for us, so that in him we might become the righteousness of God." (Obviously the "him" here is Jesus. This connects tightly with the whole theme of the book of Romans.)

Most Applicable Verse for Modern Audiences: 2 Corinthians 5:17—"Therefore, if anyone is in Christ, he is a new creation. The old has passed away; behold, the new has come" (ESV).

Theme Verse: 2 Corinthians 5:20—"We are therefore Christ's ambassadors, as though God were making his appeal through us. We implore you on Christ's behalf: Be reconciled to God."

Theme: The Holy Spirit gives believers strength to endure hard things, to serve God, and to minister to others.

If You Don't Have Time to Read the Whole Thing, at Least Read: 2 Corinthians 1 and 4.

When You Visualize 2 Corinthians, Picture: Christians repairing a church.

The Bema, judgment seat, found in Corinth.

Todd Bolen/BiblePlaces.com

VITAL STATS

Position: 48 of 66.

Chapters: 6.

Verses: 149.

Word Count: 2,230 (40/66).

Most-Used Words: Law, faith, Christ, Spirit, grace, flesh, freedom, promise, Abraham, works, slave, curse.

Group: Letters to churches.

Audience: Christians in Galatia.

Written From: Unsure. Maybe Corinth, Ephesus, or Antioch.

Date: Late 40s AD.

Popularity Rank: 24 of 66.

GALATIANS

Lightning-Fast Summary: Agitators have invaded the fledgling Gentile church in Galatia. They're preaching a different gospel and trying to get the new Christians to trust in Old Testament law for salvation. Paul writes to say that salvation is by faith, not the law, and that the Christian life is powered by the Spirit, not the law.

Unique Feature: Galatians is Paul's most intense letter. Interlopers are messing with a vulnerable church, and Paul's not having it.

The New Testament Elephant in the Room: Galatians tackles two huge questions that were obvious to people who lived in New Testament times but aren't as obvious to us: (1) Do Gentile Christians have to become Jewish to receive salvation? and (2) What will the community of faith in God look like now that it's been embraced by Gentiles with a bunch of different languages and cultures?

Who Wrote It? Paul at his feistiest.

Why He's Feisty: Paul wrote Galatians because some Jewish Christians (or Jews posing as Christians) came north from Jerusalem and told the Gentiles in Galatia that they weren't Christians if they didn't abide by the Jewish law (stuff from the Old Testament and stuff added by religious leaders after the fact). These agitators (Paul's term for them, not mine) argued that all Gentile Christians would have to be circumcised to receive salvation. Understandably, the Gentile Christians wanted to confirm that with Paul before the cutting started, and when Paul found out, he fired off this furious letter of condemnation for the outside, pro-circumcision agitators and of correction for the Galatian Christians. Paul pounds the table, reminding them all that we "have put our faith in Christ Jesus that we may be justified by faith in Christ and not by the works of the law, because by the works of the law no one will be justified" (2:16).

Circumcision Is No Joke: But that doesn't stop Paul from working in circumcision puns. When you read this letter, keep an eye out for phrases like "cut in on you" and "cut off."

Northern Ethnic Galatia: Since the 200s BC, migrants from Gaul (modern-day France) had settled in north-central Asia Minor (modern-day Turkey). By the time of Paul, this northern region had been called Galatia because of the Gauls who lived there. Though there's no record of Paul having gone there, some people think Galatians was written to churches in historic northern ethnic Galatia.

Southern Roman Galatia: Augustus became the first Roman emperor in 27 BC and immediately set about reorganizing his empire. In 25 BC, he established the official Roman province of Galatia. It included the historic ethnic northern region of the Gauls who migrated there, but it also included a southern half that wasn't ethnically Gallic (of the Gauls). The new Roman province of Galatia was unflinchingly loyal to Rome. Paul repeatedly visited four important cities there in the book of Acts (chapters 13–14). It's most likely Paul wrote Galatians to these churches he founded.

Do You Remember When We First Met and We Stoned You? Well, there *was* some stoning. When Paul did miracles, the southern Galatians in Iconium mistook him for a Greek god, so they started worshiping him. When Paul told them to stop, they stoned him until he seemed dead, and his body was dragged out of the city. But Paul shook it off and established churches across southern Galatia in Lystra, Derbe, Pisidian Antioch, and even Iconium.

At Great Cost: It makes sense that after sacrificing and suffering so much, Paul is angry that the Galatian churches are so easily fooled into believing a different gospel.

When It Was Written: If Paul was writing to the vaguely defined, historic northern ethnic region of Galatia, then Galatians was written in the mid-50s. If Paul was writing to the churches he started in Acts 13–14 in the southern part of the Roman province of Galatia, then Galatians was written in the late 40s AD, which would make it the earliest book of the New Testament.

Paul's Résumé: Paul spends chapters 1 and 2 countering accusations that the agitators made to discredit him to the Galatian church. Paul shows that he's a real apostle of Jesus, that he got the true gospel straight from Jesus, and that the original apostles in Jerusalem agreed with all that and affirmed him. The agitators are rogue agents working against the gospel and against the apostles in Jerusalem.

The Law Was Never Meant to Save: Through the middle of the book, Paul explains that the law was meant to reveal truth about God, humanity, and sin, but it's not a tool of salvation, and it never was. Paul says right standing with God has always happened by God's mercy through faith. He points to the example of Abraham, who "believed God, and it was credited to him as righteousness," and says that "those who rely on faith are blessed along with Abraham, the man of faith" (3:6–9; see Genesis 15:6).

Life by the Spirit: After taking apart the enslaving false gospel of the sharp-scalpeled circumcisers, Paul takes a gentler tone and encourages the Galatian Christians to reembrace the true gospel and live in the freedom of Christ through the Holy Spirit. He uses the metaphor of fruit to contrast life in the flesh with life in the Spirit, saying that "the fruit of the Spirit is love, joy, peace, patience, kindness, goodness, faithfulness, gentleness, self-control; against such things there is no law" (5:22–23 ESV).

Jesus Took the Curse to Break the Curse: Galatians 3:13–14—"Christ redeemed us from the curse of the law by becoming a curse for us, for it is written: 'Cursed is everyone who is hung on a pole.' He redeemed us in order that the blessing given to Abraham might come to the Gentiles through Christ Jesus, so that by faith we might receive the promise of the Spirit."

Most Shocking Moment: In Galatians 5, Paul suggests that if the agitators think circumcision, and not faith in Jesus, is what makes you right with God, then he wishes they would take that line of thinking to its logical end and "go the whole way and emasculate themselves!" (v. 12).

Most Applicable Verse for Modern Audiences: Galatians 5:13—"You, my brothers and sisters, were called to be free. But do not use your freedom to indulge the flesh; rather, serve one another humbly in love."

Theme (and Most Quoted) Verse: Galatians 2:20—"I have been crucified with Christ and I no longer live, but Christ lives in me. The life I now live in the body, I live by faith in the Son of God, who loved me and gave himself for me."

Theme/Point: The law points out sin and points to Jesus. Right standing with God happens through faith in Jesus. Christians then live by the Spirit, not the law.

If You Don't Have Time to Read the Whole Thing, at Least Read: Galatians 5, which encapsulates both the critique and the constructive proposal.

When You Visualize Galatians, Picture: Fruit.

VITAL STATS

Position: 49 of 66.
Chapters: 6.
Verses: 155.
Word Count: 2,422 (38/66).
Most-Used Words: Grace, faith, love, mystery, body, church.
Group: Letters to churches.
Audience: The church in Ephesus and Christians nearby.
Written From: House arrest in Rome.
Date: AD 62.
Popularity Rank: 11 of 66.

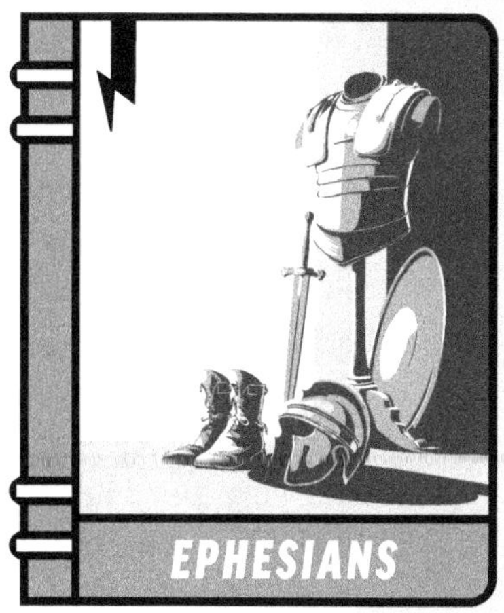

Lightning-Fast Summary: Paul is imprisoned in Rome and unsure if he'll ever make it back to see one of his favorite communities of Christians—the Ephesians—so he writes them a positive letter reminding them of the gospel and its implications in their lives.

Unique Feature: Ephesians feels like it could be written to anybody. It has only a tiny greeting on the front end and a few personal notes on the back end, and it doesn't have much in the way of situationally specific correction in the middle. Because of all that, and the general tone of the book, Ephesians is one of the easiest books in the Bible to read as though it were written to you.

Who Wrote It? Paul, while he was under fairly flexible house arrest in Rome in AD 62. This is the situation the book of Acts leaves Paul in when it wraps up.

Historical Setting: Ephesus, a wildly important port city on the west coast of Asia Minor (modern-day Turkey). It was one of the five most significant cities in the Roman world during New Testament times. It was home to the temple of Artemis (one of the seven wonders of the ancient world), and home to perhaps Paul's favorite church.

Stuff You Can Still Physically Look At: Ancient Ephesus is still there. It's a spectacular archaeological site in Turkey where you can walk the streets and see the sites from Bible times.

Did He Say It Was His Favorite? No, not explicitly, but he spent three years there, and they had some memorable adventures together, like when a silversmith named Demetrius incited a riot trying to get Paul killed (Acts 19:23–41). When it was time for Paul to face the people who wanted to kill him in Jerusalem, he lingered with the Ephesians as long as he could before they said goodbye, knowing they'd never see each other again (Acts 20:17–38). He had a soft spot for Philippi and Thessalonica too, but from the time spent, the accounts of the emotional bond, and the tone of Paul's letter to the Ephesians, there's a good case to be made that he loved them the most.

Pretty Positive for a Prisoner: Paul wrote Ephesians (as well as Philippians and Colossians) from jail, but despite his circumstances, these letters are all generally forward-looking and proactive. In the first half of Ephesians, Paul thanks God for choosing to work in the lives of the Ephesians. He gives thanks for all the most important truths of the gospel that he has written and preached about. He's grateful that God has made this people new by His grace alone, through faith alone, in Christ alone, so that no one can brag (2:8–9). And Paul is thankful that by God's power, they're no longer strangers, foreigners, and outsiders, but instead "fellow citizens with God's people and also members of his household" (2:19). The Ephesian church represents a fulfillment of the Old Testament prophets' vision of the nations coming to know and worship God.

Paul Might Die Soon, So He Wants to Say Some Stuff: What would you do if you were talking to someone you had mentored and loved for years, and you knew it might be the last time? I imagine you'd tell them you're proud of them and give them one last round of mentoring and encouragement. That's what Paul does in Ephesians 4–6. He reminds them that God's plan was always that His family of faith, drawn from all the nations, would have diverse styles and gifts to be used in the unified service of Jesus and

The Great Theater, Ephesus.
tichr/stock.adobe.com

His kingdom. He reminds them of their unity: There is "one Lord, one faith, one baptism; one God and Father of all, who is over all and through all and in all" (4:5–6).

Most Controversial Part: Some modern-day readers bristle at Ephesians 5, where Paul talks about the relationship between husbands and wives, but a closer look paints a beautiful picture. Paul likens husbands to Jesus and wives to His church. Husbands are instructed to sacrifice for their wives, even to the point of laying down their lives and their rights for them. Wives are then instructed to reciprocate this self-sacrificing attitude and behavior toward their husbands. The whole thing is clothed in love and humility.

The Armor of God: Just like in Zechariah 3, where God replaces the filthy robes of Joshua the high priest with clean robes to show God's favor, so Paul urges the church in Ephesus to take off the soiled garments of sin and pride and replace them with the attire of the virtues and values provided by Christ (chapters 4–6). And finally, Paul points to the threat of spiritual attack from the enemy and tells the Ephesians to put on the full armor of God to resist.

Theme: *New clothes, new hearts, new people.* Paul uses memorable imagery to paint a picture of Christians as God's renewed people,

His honored children, and His well-equipped agents for the good works He has prepared in advance for them to do.

Most Applicable Verses for Modern Audiences: The armor of God section in Ephesians 6:10–17.

Most Memorized Verses (You Might Want to Memorize Them Too): Ephesians 2:8–10—"For it is by grace you have been saved, through faith—and this is not from yourselves, it is the gift of God—not by works, so that no one can boast. For we are God's handiwork, created in Christ Jesus to do good works, which God prepared in advance for us to do."

If You Don't Have Time to Read the Whole Thing, at Least Read: All of Ephesians 2 and the armor of God section in Ephesians 6.

When You Visualize Ephesians, Picture: Armor.

VITAL STATS

Position: 50 of 66.
Chapters: 4.
Verses: 104.
Word Count: 1,629 (47/66).
Most-Used Words: Joy, rejoice, Christ, gospel, mind.
Group: Letters to churches.
Audience: Christians in Philippi.
Written From: House arrest in Rome.
Date: AD 60–62.
Popularity Rank: 18 of 66.

Lightning-Fast Summary: While under arrest in Rome, Paul writes to the church in Philippi to express his gratitude for them and to encourage them to live in the joy of Christ, regardless of circumstances.

Unique Feature: Philippians is a socially elegant letter. Paul gracefully navigates several challenges in four short chapters, while still somehow writing a timeless book of the Bible. Philippians is packed with razor-sharp theology wrapped in relational shrewdness and grace.

Who Wrote It? Paul, from a Roman apartment where he is under house arrest.

Historical Setting: Philippi, which was named for Alexander the Great's dad, Philip II, who founded it toward the end of the Persian era in 356 BC. It became a Roman colony as part of the fallout from the assassination of Julius Caesar in the late 40s BC. Rome settled retired soldiers from all around the empire in Philippi, which gave it a multicultural flare. Even though it was in historic Macedonia, Philippi was fiercely loyal to Rome.

Dramatic Beginnings for the Church in Philippi: Paul first visited Philippi in AD 50 as part of his second missionary journey. His visit was eventful, to say the least. There was a demon-possessed slave girl there who made money for her owner by fortune-telling. Paul drove out the demon, so the locals threw him and Silas in jail. They were singing praises to God in their cell when there was an earthquake. The cell doors opened, and the chains came off. When the jailer saw the doors, he prepared to kill himself, but Paul called out from the cell and told him not to. The jailer immediately came to belief in Jesus and asked what he had to do to be saved. Paul and Silas said, "Believe in the Lord Jesus, and you will be saved" (Acts 16:31).

What's Happening Now? About ten years and three missionary journeys later, the Philippian church took up a collection for Paul when they heard about his arrest and sent it to Rome with a member of their church named Epaphroditus. Paul, who needed support to sustain himself while under house arrest, was relieved and encouraged. He sends the letter we call Philippians back to Philippi with Epaphroditus to say thanks, to reassure them of their friend's well-being, and to address a few important issues for them as a church.

There's a Problem, and We'll Get to That Eventually: Things in Philippi are going pretty well, but Paul is aware of a problem between two women who've been quarreling. Rather than going right at the issue, Paul first exuberantly thanks the Philippian believers for their gift and for who they are as a church. He tells them he rejoices that his chains are advancing the gospel, and says he wants Christ to be exalted in his life, whether he lives or whether he dies. Paul writes, "For to me, to live is Christ and to die is gain" (1:21).

Hymn to Christ: In chapter 2, Paul shares a hymn to Christ. It celebrates the incarnation as Jesus' work and praises it as an act of humility and obedience to God the Father. This is the most important part of this book and one of the most important parts of the whole Bible. Every point Paul wants to make in Philippians flows out of the passage that says Jesus, who was in His nature God, "did not consider equality with God something to be used to his own advantage; rather, he made himself nothing by taking the very nature of a servant, being made in human likeness" (2:6–7).

That's What We Take Our Cues From: Paul explains that Christ's example should inform everything in the life of the Christian and the church. Whether we're serving and thanking each other, suffering, working, worshiping, singing, or working out ongoing disputes that have been hurting the church, it's all supposed be done in imitation of Christ's humility. Over the course of the book, Paul deftly weaves gentle correction, gratitude, and reassurance into a profound declaration of the gospel.

Most Applicable Verses for Modern Audiences: These are both about enduring and being joyful in all circumstances. Philippians 4:4—"Rejoice in the Lord always. I will say it again: Rejoice!" and Philippians 4:13—"I can do all things through him who strengthens me" (ESV).

If You Don't Have Time to Read the Whole Thing, at Least Read: The hymn to Christ and the run-up to it in Philippians 2:1–11.

When You Visualize Philippians, Picture: A gift for a prisoner.

Traditional site of Paul's prison in Philippi.

Todd Bolen/BiblePlaces.com

VITAL STATS

Position: 51 of 66.
Chapters: 4.
Verses: 95.
Word Count: 1,582 (49/66).
Most-Used Words: Christ, God, Lord, body, faith, love, wisdom.
Group: Letters to churches.
Audience: Christians in Colossae.
Written From: House arrest in Rome.
Date: AD 60–62.
Popularity Rank: 28 of 66.

COLOSSIANS

Lightning-Fast Summary: Paul writes to the Christians in Colossae, challenging them to resist mixing fashionable, local pagan thought with Christian faith, and instead worship only Jesus, who is supreme over everything.

Unique Feature: Colossians may be the least familiar of Paul's letters. It and Romans are the only two of his books that aren't directed to churches he founded. As a result, the tone is far less familiar than his other letters to churches.

Who Wrote It? Paul, who is under house arrest in Rome.

When It Was Written: Paul probably wrote Ephesians, Philippians, Philemon, and Colossians during his relatively flexible confinement to an apartment in Rome from AD 60–62.

Historical Setting: Colossae was a power player in the age of Persia (550–330 BC), but hundreds of years later, during New Testament times, it was a modest city that was bigger in name and reputation than in actual size or influence. Colossae sits inland, about a hundred miles west of Ephesus in Asia Minor (modern-day Turkey). Acts 19:10 makes it clear that Paul's preaching during his time in Ephesus had a ripple effect throughout the region. People came to the grand city of Ephesus, believed in Jesus, and then took the message back home with them to found Christian communities like the one in Colossae.

Paul's History with Colossae: There's no evidence that Paul ever went to Colossae or started a church there. When Paul taught in Ephesus, a Colossian named Epaphras became a Christian and then took the gospel back to Colossae. He's one of three people there who Paul seems to know. Other than that connection, Paul is writing this letter on reputation alone, with no previous history or miraculous moments to lend him credibility with this struggling church.

Courier: An associate of Paul's named Tychicus delivered the letter to Colossae. Onesimus, a runaway slave who became a Christian when he met Paul in Rome, was with him and probably carrying the letter of Philemon.

Why the Letter? Nobody knows exactly what was wrong with the Colossian church, but from Paul's letter, we can figure out that the problems were theological. When the Greeks and Romans encountered new gods, they'd often simply roll them into their already existing pantheon and mix all the rituals, morals, and beliefs together to form an ever-evolving hybrid religion. It looks like that's what was happening in Colossae, and Paul is writing to say that Christ alone is supreme, and so all the old pagan business has to be rejected completely.

The Heart of the Letter: Just like everything in Philippians flows out of the hymn to Christ (2:6–11), so everything in Colossians flows out of a grand declaration of Christ's supremacy in chapter 1. There's no point in keeping any lingering vestiges of pagan gods when Jesus is:

- the image of the invisible God (1:15);
- the maker of everything—including Aristotle's visible world and Plato's invisible world (1:16);
- the establisher of all governments and authorities (1:16);
- the One who holds everything together—another nod to Greek philosophical assumptions about the nature of all things (1:17);
- the head of the church (1:18);

- the firstborn from the dead (1:18);
- God in the flesh (1:19);
- the solver of the human problem and the vanquisher of death (1:20);
- the purifier of the sinful (1:22); and
- the healer of the relationship between God and human beings (1:22–23).

Most Applicable Verse for Modern Audiences: Colossians 3:23—"Whatever you do, work at it with all your heart, as working for Lord, not for human masters."

Most Famous Verse: Colossians 3:12 is a hybrid of Galatians' fruit of the Spirit section and Ephesians' section about putting on the new self—"Therefore, as God's chosen people, holy and dearly loved, clothe yourselves with compassion, kindness, humility, gentleness and patience."

Theme Verse: Colossians 1:15—"The Son is the image of the invisible God, the firstborn over all creation."

Theme: Jesus isn't simply one more regional god to be added to a collection of pagan deities; He is God in the flesh and supreme over all.

If You Don't Have Time to Read the Whole Thing, at Least Read: The supremacy of Christ section in Colossians 1:15–23.

When You Visualize Colossians, Picture: Jesus casually musing at a crumbled pagan colossus.

VITAL STATS

Position: 52 of 66.
Chapters: 5.
Verses: 89.
Word Count: 1,481 (50/66).
Most-Used Words: God, Lord, Jesus, faith, love, we, brothers, hope, coming, day, sanctification.
Group: Letters to churches.
Audience: Christians in Thessalonica.
Written From: Probably Corinth, not too long after Paul got run out of Thessalonica.
Date: AD 51.
Popularity Rank: 36 of 66.

1 THESSALONIANS

Lightning-Fast Summary: Paul started the church in Thessalonica but had to flee because of persecution. Now he's writing to embolden the Christians there in the face of persecution and to urge them to remember that Jesus will return someday.

Unique Feature: By this author's count, the word *we* appears sixty-two times in the book of 1 Thessalonians, but the word *I* appears only five times.

Why No I? First Thessalonians is presented as being written by Paul, Silas, and Timothy together. When Paul specifically wants to talk about himself in chapter 2, he goes out of his way to say, "For we wanted to come to you—certainly I, Paul, did, again and again" (v. 18).

In It Together: The we language makes perfect sense because Paul, Silas, Timothy, and the Thessalonian church had a short but dramatic history together, and presenting the letter as a group project would make it clear to them that Paul hadn't abandoned them during hard times, nor lazily pawned them off to Timothy.

Historical Setting: Thessalonica, which in Paul's time was the cosmopolitan capital of the Roman province of Macedonia. The Macedonian name still carried clout from the achievements of Alexander the Great, but the pagan city was now staunchly loyal to Rome.

Arrested Development: On his second missionary journey (Acts 17), Paul shows up in Thessalonica. He preaches at the Jewish synagogue there for a few weeks, and Jews and Gentiles alike respond. The message particularly hits home with the influential women of the city. It looks like Paul and Silas are going to be there for a long time so they can properly establish a church in this strategic and receptive location. However, some Jews who don't like Paul's message gather ruffians and spark a riot in the middle of town. The rioters can't find Paul and Silas, so they drag Jason (who hosted Paul) in front of the city officials and accuse the Christians of trying to establish Jesus as a rival king to Caesar. Paul and Silas have to flee the city at night and aren't able to finish training the new Christians in Thessalonica.

So You'd Figure Their Church Would Fail: But you'd be wrong. Paul stations Timothy in Thessalonica to finish training the church—a smart move, because the angry people there won't recognize him. With Timothy's help, the persecuted church in Thessalonica not only survives but thrives.

Picking Up Where We Left Off: Paul (and in a way, Silas and Timothy) starts by reminding the Thessalonian Christians that God chose them "in the midst of severe suffering" (1 Thessalonians 1:6). He tells them they're a model to other Christians when it comes to dealing with persecution and suffering. In chapters 2–3, Paul thanks God for them and for the way they responded when he brought the message of Jesus to Thessalonica. He tells them he misses them and is encouraged by what Timothy is reporting about them.

What Happens to Dead Christians? The Thessalonians want to know what happens to Christians who've died (chapter 4). That's a natural question for anyone to ask, and even more natural for persecuted Christians. In the final two chapters, Paul speaks to this question in terms of the unfolding of God's grand redemptive plan.

The Day of the Lord: Like most of the Old Testament prophets, Paul says the day of the Lord is coming. Sometimes that term means terrifying judgment, and sometimes it means glorious deliverance. Here Paul pictures a beautiful scene where Jesus comes on the clouds and His followers, both living and dead, meet Him in the air and be with the Lord forever (4:17). Whether you live to see it or die before that day, Paul says, you're all fully going to be a part of it.

Echoing Jesus' teaching in Matthew 24–25, Paul tells the Thessalonians to stay ready for this moment, but also to endure.

Some Controversy Here, but Jesus' Return Is What Matters: Some say Paul is describing Jesus coming to collect His followers to be with Him in heaven at the end of all things, and others think this scene happens just before Jesus reigns on earth for an age. But Paul doesn't treat it like a controversy or something to be fought over at all. He treats Jesus' return in that moment as a source of joy, hope, and comfort in a time of suffering.

Most Applicable Verses for Modern Audiences: 1 Thessalonians 5:16–18—"Rejoice always, pray continually, give thanks in all circumstances; for this is God's will for you in Christ Jesus."

Theme Verses: 1 Thessalonians 4:17–18—"And so we will be with the Lord forever. Therefore encourage one another with these words."

Theme: Keep living godly lives while you wait for Christ's return.

If You Don't Have Time to Read the Whole Thing, at Least Read: 1 Thessalonians 4.

When You Visualize 1 Thessalonians, Picture: Christians meeting Jesus in the air.

2 THESSALONIANS

VITAL STATS

Position: 53 of 66.
Chapters: 3.
Verses: 47.
Word Count: 823 (60/66).
Most-Used Words: Lord, God, Jesus, brothers and sisters, coming, faith, glory, day.
Group: Letters to churches.
Audience: Christians in Thessalonica.
Written From: Corinth.
Date: AD 51.
Popularity Rank: 49 of 66.

Lightning-Fast Summary : The Thessalonians are a church under duress. They hope that Jesus will come back soon, and rumors circulate saying He already did and they missed it. Paul writes to clear up those rumors and strengthen them for the long haul.

Unique Feature: Both of these letters to the Thessalonians are the first-century equivalent of a quick, back-and-forth email thread. First, the Thessalonians had Timothy deliver a message to Paul, then Paul writes them back in what we call 1 Thessalonians, then they must have mailed Paul more questions, so then Paul answers those questions with what we call 2 Thessalonians.

Which Is Why It Feels Different: In a series of back-and-forth emails, the personal stuff mostly happens in the first message, and after that, the messages get shorter to work out the details. It's the same with 1 and 2 Thessalonians. The first book is heartfelt and personal. That makes sense, because it's the first time they've talked since things turned insane in Thessalonica and Paul and Silas had to flee under cover of darkness. Now that they've caught up, this second book is way quicker and more direct. Compared to the first letter, it might sound curt, but they're well into a productive conversation at this point and are prioritizing efficiency now that they've greeted and reassured each other.

Historical Setting: Thessalonica, the proudly Roman capital of Macedonia, received the message of Jesus positively at first, but after a few weeks, agitators enlisted rioters to poison public mood toward Paul and the gospel. Paul fled the city but deployed Timothy to bolster the persecuted church there.

Postmark: Paul wrote this from Corinth during his eighteen-month stay. Corinth was a high-maintenance church for Paul, and the reader gets the sense that Paul might prefer to be in Thessalonica.

Things Are Still Tough: Paul clearly received a report that the Thessalonians' situation hasn't improved. They're still being persecuted and are confused about Christ's return, and maybe related to that, some of them have lost their work ethic. Second Thessalonians directly addresses all that.

Don't Quit: Paul tells the church to hang on and trust in God's justice. They're participating in the kingdom of God through their suffering (1:1–12).

You Didn't Miss It: Paul reassures the Thessalonians that, despite rumors to the contrary, they haven't missed Jesus' return. In Matthew 24, Jesus' disciples know He is about to be killed by the religious leaders, so, just like the Thessalonians, they start poking around the question of how they'll know when He's coming back. The gist of what Jesus says is this: "Don't think every hard thing that happens in the world is the end of things. Instead, stay ready like I'm coming back any minute, but plan and endure like it might be a long time. Also, don't worry; when I do come back, you won't be able to miss it." (This is a heavy paraphrase of all of Matthew 24–25.) Paul's practical exhortation to the Thessalonians is the same.

The Man of Lawlessness: To show them they haven't missed Jesus, Paul tells them a little bit more about all that has to happen before Jesus returns. In chapter 2, he describes a man of lawlessness who'll set himself up in God's temple. His exact identity is debated, but what's certain is that he's a powerful, prideful enemy of God and His people. His actions are reminiscent of Daniel's ancient prophecy about an "abomination that causes desolation" (11:31), which Jesus references in Matthew 24:15. Paul says the man of lawlessness will fool tons of people and cause major problems, but Jesus will overthrow him (2 Thessalonians 2:1–12).

Stand Firm: Paul challenges the Thessalonians to stand firm in the face of evil while God's redemptive plan unfolds. To do that, they'll need to hold fast to what they've been taught about Jesus (2:15).

No Work, No Eat: Finally, Paul rebukes some Christians in Thessalonica who have lost their work ethic. He tells the rest to avoid such people and let them feel ashamed of their laziness as a way of helping them (3:10–14).

Theme Verse: The Thessalonians can't control the unfolding of history by obsessing to the point of paralysis over the timeline of God's redemptive plan, but they can live proactive, expectant, holy lives. Second Thessalonians 3:13 captures that idea—"And as for you, brothers and sisters, never tire of doing what is good."

Theme: Keep living active, godly lives while you wait for Christ's return.

If You Don't Have Time to Read the Whole Thing, at Least Read: 2 Thessalonians 2.

When You Visualize 2 Thessalonians, Picture: The man of lawlessness.

Agora ruins in Thessalonica.

ppl/Shutterstock.com

VITAL STATS

Position: 54 of 66.
Chapters: 6.
Verses: 113.
Word Count: 1,591 (48/66).
Most-Used Words: Faith, doctrine, godliness, good, teach, truth, love, savior, command, Jesus, sound.
Group: Pastoral Letters.
Audience: Timothy (in Ephesus).
Written From: Probably Macedonia.
Date: AD 64.
Popularity Rank: 32 of 66.

Lightning-Fast Summary : Paul writes a coaching letter to his protégé, telling him how best to help the church in Ephesus.

Unique Feature: Every letter in the New Testament up to this point was written by Paul to Christians in a city or region. First Timothy is different. It's written to one person and feels far more familiar and personal than any of the other letters so far.

Pastoral Letters: Both of the letters to Timothy and the one to Titus are all personal letters to Christian leaders Paul is mentoring and increasingly depending on to spread the gospel. These three books are called the Pastoral Letters or the Pastoral Epistles.

Who's Timothy? Paul met Timothy in Lystra (a Roman colony in Galatia) on his second missionary journey. Timothy's mom was a Jewish Christian, and his dad was Greek. Timothy was well positioned to blend in socially and talk with anyone because he was a Greek Jewish Christian from a Roman colony. He came highly recommended and made a good impression, so Paul and Silas enlisted Timothy as part of their team. That turned out to be the right call. Timothy was smart, reliable, and willing to serve wherever needed without complaining. Paul could dispatch him into challenging situations and expect good results (like in Philippi or Thessalonica).

But Now We're Talking About Ephesus: Paul wrote 1 Timothy because his protégé was facing his biggest challenge to date. He was with the Christians in Ephesus trying to sort out big problems, with big stakes, in a big church, full of big personalities, situated in a big city.

Where It Was Written: First Timothy 1:3 hints strongly that Paul was writing from Macedonia. He had been released from his two-year house arrest in Rome in AD 62 and likely embarked on a fourth missionary journey that happened after the book of Acts. Paul had been saying for years that he wanted to take the gospel to Spain, and if that was his destination, he wouldn't have wanted to backtrack from Macedonia to deal with the problems in Ephesus in person. In 1 Timothy, Paul is making sure Timothy has what he needs to fix things in Ephesus.

What's Wrong in Ephesus? Lots. False teachers have infiltrated the church and many are starting to obsess about the Old Testament laws and the genealogies in counterproductive ways. (See the Historical Setting section in the Ephesians chapter for context.) There's pride and greed, as well as feuding. Ephesus has been a great church for a long time, but this wasn't her best moment.

Commissioning: Paul thanks Jesus for commissioning him to carry the gospel. He also makes sure Timothy is clear on his objective in Ephesus: Stop the false teachers and get the church back on track. Paul singles out two particularly pernicious false teachers named Hymenaeus and Alexander.

Getting Ephesus on Track: Over the next couple chapters, Paul gives Timothy a specific list of stuff to focus on. He wants their worship to be humble and orderly, and he wants the brash, wealthy women of the church to quit flaunting their riches and influence and instead be modest, clothing themselves with "good deeds" (2:10). He also wants Timothy to clean up the leadership situation. Paul expects officeholders in the church to be people of temperance and dignity. Apparently, the false teachers had convinced people that getting married and eating meat are forbidden by God, and Paul wants Timothy to nip that nonsense in the bud. Timothy will also need to reform how the church ministers to widows, as well as the priorities of some of the elders.

It's a tough list, but Paul has good practical and theological rationales for all of it, and he's confident that Timothy can get the job done.

Important Jesus Verses: 1 Timothy 2:5–6—"For there is one God and one mediator between God and mankind, the man Christ Jesus, who gave himself as a ransom for all people."

Most Famous Verse: 1 Timothy 1:15—"Here is a trustworthy saying that deserves full acceptance: Christ Jesus came into the world to save sinners—of whom I am the worst."

Theme Verse: 1 Timothy 4:12—"Don't let anyone look down on you because you are young, but set an example for the believers in speech, in conduct, in love, in faith and in purity."

Theme: The Ephesian church is looking silly and dumb in front of their neighbors. Paul sends Timothy, and this letter, to get that straightened out for the well-being of the Ephesian Christians, for the credibility of their witness to their community, and for the glory of God.

If You Don't Have Time to Read the Whole Thing, at Least Read: 1 Timothy 4:6–16.

When You Visualize 1 Timothy, Picture: Brave young Timothy.

2 TIMOTHY

VITAL STATS

Position: 55 of 66.
Chapters: 4.
Verses: 83.
Word Count: 1,238 (53/66).
Most-Used Words: God, Christ, faith, truth, gospel, suffer.
Group: Pastoral Letters.
Audience: Timothy (in Ephesus).
Written From: Paul's final imprisonment in Rome.
Date: AD 65–67.
Popularity Rank: 31 of 66.

Lightning-Fast Summary: Paul is in a Roman prison waiting to be executed, so he writes to his protégé and friend Timothy asking him to visit one last time before the end and encouraging him to carry on the work after Paul is gone.

Unique Feature: Second Timothy contains Paul's last words in the Bible. He was beheaded in Rome at the order of Emperor Nero not long after he wrote it.

Who's Timothy? Timothy was a young man Paul constantly counted on to help him build the church around the whole Roman world. There's more about him in the previous chapter.

Stuff You Can Still Physically Look At: The Mamertine Prison in Rome where Paul wrote 2 Timothy. It would have been an especially dank, dark, cold, and lonely place to live out your last days. Paul asks Timothy to bring him his favorite coat if he comes to visit, and when you're standing in that cell, you can see why.

What Would You Say? If you knew it was almost over and you had time to write to someone you love? Paul had plenty of time to think about it, and he had a lot to say:

Mamertine prison, Rome.

Pablo Debat/stock.adobe.com

- He calls Timothy "my dear son" and reflects on the family legacy of faith that Timothy will carry forward (1:1–3).
- He explains the gospel, even though Timothy already knows it, and tells Timothy not to be ashamed of it (1:6–14).
- He says he's hurt by those who abandoned him and encouraged by those who didn't (1:15–18).
- He explains the gospel again, even though Timothy still knows it, and tells Timothy to be willing to suffer for it (2:1–14).
- He tells Timothy not to get sucked into youthful mistakes and dumb gossip, but instead to "present yourself to God as one approved, a worker who does not need to be ashamed and who correctly handles the word of truth" (2:15).
- He warns Timothy that false teachers will keep saying what people want to hear. Paul's advice? Don't fall for it, and keep opposing them (3:1–17).
- He urges Timothy to keep learning and teaching the Scriptures "in season and out of season," because Scripture is useful for "teaching, rebuking, correcting and training in righteousness" (4:2; 3:16).

- He wants Timothy to know he's happy with how he has used his life: "I have fought the good fight, I have finished the race, I have kept the faith" (4:7).
- He takes his own language from the book of Romans and uses it show Timothy what it looks like to face death clothed in true theology. Paul writes, "Now there is in store for me the crown of righteousness, which the Lord, the righteous Judge, will award to me on that day" (4:8).
- He passes along final greetings, final heartaches, and asks for his scrolls and his coat—because it was cold (4:9–18).

Theme: The last leg of Paul's race was to embolden Timothy to keep running.

When You Visualize 2 Timothy, Picture: Paul's coat.

VITAL STATS

Position: 56 of 66.
Chapters: 3.
Verses: 46.
Word Count: 659 (61/66).
Most-Used Words: God, good, faith, teach, truth, works.
Group: Pastoral Letters.
Audience: Titus (in Crete).
Written From: Maybe Macedonia or Nicopolis.
Date: AD 63 or 64ish.
Popularity Rank: 48 of 66.

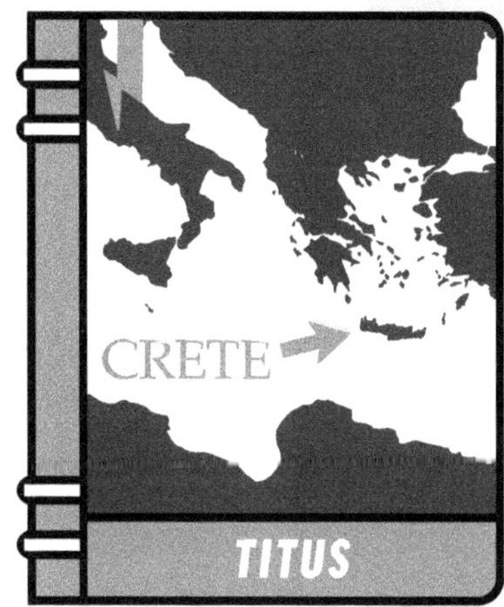

TITUS

Lightning-Fast Summary: Paul dispatches Titus to the island of Crete to strengthen the church there. It's not long before the Cretans begin living up to their notorious reputation, so Paul writes Titus with guidance on how to get the Christian community on track.

Unique Feature: Titus was an important figure in the early church and a key ally of Paul, but he isn't mentioned at all in the book of Acts. Everything we know about him comes from this book, church traditions, and about ten other mentions in various New Testament letters.

Chronology: The letters of Paul aren't arranged chronologically, so it can feel a little odd reading the Bible straight through for the first time—you get done saying goodbye to Paul in 2 Timothy, and then you turn the page to Titus and Paul is fine. Obviously, Titus predates 2 Timothy.

Who Wrote It? Paul.

Who's Titus? Titus was a Greek Christian who appears on the scene just after Paul's first missionary journey. He and Timothy are always closely linked, so it's possible that Titus was from somewhere near Timothy's hometown of Lystra in Galatia (modern-day Turkey). In Galatians

2, Paul says he brought Titus to the Jerusalem Council (Acts 15), probably as proof that Gentiles were becoming Christians and receiving the Holy Spirit. From there on out, Titus goes with Paul on his travels, delivers letters like 2 Corinthians, and is dispatched to help struggling churches get on their feet.

Historical Setting: Centuries before anyone had ever heard of Rome, the island of Crete was home to a dominant naval civilization called the Minoans. Even as their power faded, Crete's unique identity persisted. But it wasn't the most flattering identity. One of their own philosophers, a man named Epimenides, famously said, "Cretans are always liars, evil brutes, lazy gluttons" (1:12). Whether he meant it or whether he was just playing a paradoxical philosophy game, the charge rang true for centuries either way. To be a Cretan was to be silly, uncultured, and dishonest.

The Cretan Church: After Paul was released from his house arrest in Rome, he went back to what he had been doing. Smart people argue that he embarked on a fourth and even a fifth missionary journey that aren't recorded in the Bible. Whether any kind of journeys rising to that level occurred or not, it looks like Paul found time to start a church on Crete and then left Titus there to get it fully established. It wasn't long after Paul left—and the Cretan Christians started acting like Cretans—that Titus wrote to Paul for advice. The letter to Titus is Paul's response to that.

On-the-Go Reply: Paul's greeting to Titus is warm and generous but also short. Paul was probably arrested for the final time shortly after writing this letter, and he may have been scrambling to get in as much work and correspondence as possible before Rome would come calling again. When Paul did get arrested for the final time, it was apparently so abrupt that he couldn't grab his scrolls or even his coat (because he had to ask for them at the end of 2 Timothy).

Crete Needs Reputable Leaders: In the spirit of getting down to business, Paul is already talking about character expectations for church leaders by verse 6. Titus should only appoint elders who have their households in order. They have to be men of solid reputation and self-control.

Fair Havens, Crete.

Todd Bolen/BiblePlaces.com

Paul Quotes Epimenides: At this point in his life, Paul has had his fill of false teachers infiltrating and wrecking these fledgling churches. Agitators like the ones who plagued the Galatian church were pushing the Cretans away from the gospel and toward faith in the Jewish law for salvation. Paul had already addressed this in great detail in Galatians, and with that established, he tells Titus not to tolerate these false teachers at all. Paul likens them to the worst expressions of Cretan culture by quoting Crete's own Epimenides, who called them liars, brutes, and gluttons (1:12, quoted on previous page). Then Paul declares that the saying is true and that Titus should rebuke them.

Getting It Right: Paul tells Titus to teach truth and set an example for the young men to follow. Titus's job is to stabilize things and to get the Cretans to live peacefully and to abandon their embarrassing chaotic behavior. The Cretan Christians are supposed to be the exact opposite of the historical reputation of their people; they are to live like sons and daughters of Jesus the King.

Theme: Titus is meant to confront low-character nonsense and false teaching and instill right Christian living in the church, and the reader should follow suit.

All of Titus in One Crucial Passage: Titus 2:11–15 covers Titus's mission, the gospel, the full divinity of Jesus, and right Christian living all in a few phenomenal phrases. Here it is:

> For the grace of God has appeared that offers salvation to all people. It teaches us to say "No" to ungodliness and worldly passions, and to live self-controlled, upright and godly lives in this present age, while we wait for the blessed hope—the appearing of the glory of our great God and Savior, Jesus Christ, who gave himself for us to redeem us from all wickedness and to purify for himself a people that are his very own, eager to do what is good.
>
> These, then, are the things you should teach. Encourage and rebuke with all authority. Do not let anyone despise you.

When You Visualize Titus, Picture: The flat, skinny island of Crete.

VITAL STATS

Position: 57 of 66.
Chapters: 1.
Verses: 25.
Word Count: 335 (64/66).
Most-Used Words: Lord, Christ, Jesus, chains, brother, slave, love.
Group: Pastoral Letters.
Audience: Philemon and the Colossian church.
Written From: House arrest in Rome.
Date: AD 60–62.
Popularity Rank: 65 of 66.

Lightning-Fast Summary: Onesimus is a runaway slave who became a Christian when he met Paul in Rome. Paul asks the man's master, Philemon, to receive Onesimus back as a Christian brother.

Unique Feature: This tiny book was revolutionary when it came out. No one actively challenged the institution of slavery in the Roman world; it was an accepted fact of life. In Philemon, Paul doesn't posture with some impotent, hollow rhetoric critiquing slavery. He does something much bigger. In the name of Christ and the gospel, Paul asks Philemon to forego punishing his runaway slave, and receive him back as a brother. Paul's request elevates Christian brotherhood above all other social statuses and represents a challenge to the ancient institution of slavery.

Who Wrote It? Paul.

Two Books at Once: Onesimus carried the letter we call Philemon to Colossae. He traveled there with another one of Paul's coworkers, Tychicus, who carried the letter we call Colossians with him.

That's a Lot of Bible for a Church Paul Didn't Visit: Well, maybe he did, but there's no record of Paul ever setting foot in Colossae. The church there was an offshoot of the Ephesian church about a hundred miles down the road. Paul knew a few people in Colossae, including Philemon, but he wasn't tight with the church like he was with the Corinthians or the Ephesians.

Did You Guys Hear That I'm in Jail? If Paul has to be in jail, he's going to make sure Philemon and the Colossian church know it. Paul mentions he's in jail in literally 20 percent of the verses in this book. Paul's asking Philemon to do something difficult, and he wants to make sure Philemon knows he isn't asking from a position of comfort. Paul is making sacrifices too.

Philemon and Onesimus: Philemon is mentioned only in this short book in the New Testament as a wealthy Christian from Colossae who owned slaves. Onesimus met Paul in Rome and became a Christian. Paul was impressed with Onesimus's talent and was sad to have to send him back to Colossae. Unfortunately, we don't get the details of Onesimus's conversion, nor do we know for sure whether Philemon honored Paul's request.

How Did It Work Out? The Bible doesn't say, but Ignatius of Antioch talks about a man named Onesimus being the bishop of Ephesus around AD 100. If that's the same guy, then he went from slave, to fugitive, to convert, to gospel ambassador in Rome, to returned slave, to freed slave, to brother, to elder, to bishop, to saint. His life illustrates the paradigm-wrecking power of Jesus and the gospel described in Paul's letter to the Galatians: "There is neither Jew nor Gentile, neither slave nor free, nor is there male and female, for you are all one in Christ Jesus" (3:28).

I'm Asking You Nicely: This may be the simplest book in the Bible. Paul says hello, lets everyone know (*many* times) that he's making this request from jail, and then thanks God for Philemon. After that Paul vouches for Onesimus as a brother and a gifted servant of Christ. Paul asks Philemon to forgive Onesimus for running away and receive him as a brother. Paul even seems to intone Philemon might free Onesimus altogether, which was unthinkable in the ancient world under those circumstances. If there's any outstanding debt or if Onesimus owes Philemon anything, Paul says he'll pay it himself. Finally, Paul sends along an influential hello from Epaphras, who founded the church in Colossae and is in jail with Paul in Rome.

Theme: The gospel upsets the normal social order of things. It makes true forgiveness possible. It creates a new family of faith among Jesus' followers.

Theme Verse: Philemon verse 16—" . . . no longer as a slave, but better than a slave, as a dear brother."

When You Visualize Philemon, Picture: Onesimus the slave returning home.

VITAL STATS

Position: 58 of 66.
Chapters: 13.
Verses: 303.
Word Count: 4,953 (31/66).
Most-Used Words: Faith, better, covenant, priest, promise, sacrifice, eternal.
Group: General Letters.
Audience: Jewish Christians everywhere.
Written From: Unknown.
Date: AD 60s (before AD 70).
Popularity Rank: 15 of 66.

HEBREWS

Lightning-Fast Summary: A letter showing that Jesus is superior to everything and over everything. He is God, and readers should follow Him exclusively.

Unique Feature: Hebrews is a letter, but it's basically all business. There's no opening greeting. It immediately jumps into important stuff about Jesus, and then it's wall-to-wall theology until the last couple of lines, where there's a brief general sign-off.

The previous thirteen books of the New Testament (all letters from Paul) are deeply relational and closely tied to Paul's work and personality. Hebrews isn't like that. It's a hardcore theology treatise that mostly keeps the author and his circumstances in the background.

So Much Old Testament: Hebrews directly quotes the Old Testament at a higher rate than any other New Testament book.

Who Wrote It? Only God knows. Unlike all of Paul's letters, it is unsigned and has very few biographical clues. We can deduce that the author was a man (from grammatical hints), that he was well connected and respected in the church, that he knew Timothy, that he never met Jesus, that he was very likely Jewish, and that he had elite-level mastery of the Old Testament. Apollos and Barnabas are popular guesses, and some say it was Paul writing in a style different from his usual one.

When It Was Written: Hebrews talks about religious activities as though they're still going on, which puts the date before AD 70 (when the Romans destroyed the temple).

Original Audience: The second to last verse reads, "Those from Italy send you their greetings" (13:24). This could mean the letter was sent to Christians in Rome, and traveling Romans were sending greetings back home (in which case this could be titled 2 Romans?). Or it could mean Hebrews was written from Italy to somewhere else. Either way, Hebrews is a great title for the book because it's clearly targeted to a Jewish-Christian audience. The author assumes his readers know the Old Testament well and makes no effort whatsoever to explain Jewish stuff.

What Does Jesus Mean for Judaism? In the early going of Jesus' ministry, you can tell a question is percolating in the minds of the Jews who find Him compelling. Basically they were thinking, *This seems true and real, but we already have a religion. What does Jesus mean for Judaism?* Jesus speaks to that in Matthew 5:17: "Do not think that I have come to abolish the Law or the Prophets; I have not come to abolish them but to fulfill them." Hebrews was meant to help Jewish Christians get the answer to this question on lockdown by showing that Jesus is the superior completion of everything they know and believe in from the Old Testament.

How It's Built: The first ten chapters of Hebrews are made of four blocks proving that Jesus is superior to angels, Moses, priests, and the sacrificial system. The last three chapters take this to its logical conclusion for the readers, showing how Jesus perfectly completes the point of those four blocks from the Old Testament and concluding that Christians should endure hardship and faithfully follow only Jesus.

Prologue and Thesis: Hebrews opens by declaring that Jesus is the "radiance of God's glory and the exact representation of his being, sustaining all things by his powerful word" (1:3). Five verses later, the author doubles down on the divinity of Christ, quoting

Psalm 45:6: "But about the Son he says, 'Your throne, O God, will last for ever and ever; a scepter of justice will be the scepter of your kingdom.'" Jesus, who is God the Son, has more power and authority and a greater role than angels, Moses, priests, and sacrifices.

Stuff Jesus Is Superior To: Hebrews 1–4 are about how Jesus is the perfect messenger of God—better even than the angels whom Jewish tradition said delivered the law to Moses. Chapters 3–4 say Jesus is the perfect leader for God's people—better even than Moses. Chapters 4–7 show how Jesus is the perfect reconciler between God and mankind—better even than the Old Testament priests. Chapters 8–10 portray Jesus as the perfect, permanent sacrifice powerful enough to cover every sin ever committed—better even than the entire sacrificial system.

By Faith: The final section starts in chapter 11 and runs to the end of the book. Here the author of Hebrews lists a bunch of the great characters from the Old Testament and shows that faith is what they got right and the attribute they had in common. Then in chapter 12, he urges the reader, in light of all those great people of faith from ages past, to set aside sin and competing loyalties, "fixing our eyes on Jesus, the pioneer and perfecter of faith. For the joy set before him he endured the cross, scorning its shame, and sat down at the right hand of the throne of God" (12:2).

Most Famous Passage: The Hall of Fame of Faith in chapter 11 (usually just called the Hall of Faith). It's a who's who of the Old Testament that echoes Paul's point in Galatians—that even in the Old Testament, people had right standing with God through faith.

Most Memorable, Important Verse About the Bible: Hebrews 4:12—"For the word of God is alive and active. Sharper than any double-edged sword, it penetrates even to dividing soul and spirit, joints and marrow; it judges the thoughts and attitudes of the heart."

Bridge Between the Old and New Testaments: If you want to sort out the question of how the Old Testament and New Testament fit together and what Jesus means when He says He fulfills the Law and the Prophets, read Matthew, then Acts 10–15, then Galatians, then Hebrews. It'll help.

Theme and Theme Verse: Hebrews 12:1—"Therefore, since we are surrounded by such a great cloud of witnesses, let us throw off everything that hinders and the sin that so easily entangles. And let us run with perseverance the race marked out for us."

When You Visualize Hebrews, Picture: A Hall of Fame.

VITAL STATS

Position: 59 of 66.
Chapters: 5.
Verses: 108.
Word Count: 1,742 (45/66).
Most-Used Words: Faith, works, law, tongue, wisdom, brother.
Group: General Letters.
Audience: Jewish Christians everywhere.
Written From: Jerusalem.
Date: Before AD 62, but probably the late 40s AD.
Popularity Rank: 20 of 66.

JAMES

Lightning-Fast Summary: A letter reminding Christians that right belief in Christ should produce Christlike actions.

Unique Feature: The book of James was likely written by the James who was the half brother of Jesus.

General Letters: Christians call the last seven letters of the New Testament the General Letters (or General Epistles). These include James, Peter's letters, John's letters, and Jude. Sometimes Hebrews is lumped in with this group, but Revelation is always treated separately. Unlike Paul's thirteen letters written to specific churches or specific individuals, the General Letters were written by several authors to a broad audience, and they deal with big-picture questions.

Who Wrote It? There are a handful of Jameses in the New Testament, but James the Just (the half brother of Jesus) fits the bill for being the author of this letter. He wasn't sure what to make of Jesus' ministry in the early going (John 7) but became a Christian after his brother's death and resurrection. James was revered as the leader of the Jerusalem church, and he presided over the Jerusalem Council in Acts 15, rendering the final ruling that "we should not make it difficult for the Gentiles who are turning to God" (v. 19). According to early Jewish and Christian sources, he was martyred in Jerusalem around AD 62.

When It Was Written: James couldn't have written the book after AD 62, for obvious reasons. However, it's possible that James might be one of the earliest books of the New Testament. There are internal hints that the church was in an early stage of its development. There's no mention of the Gentile question, and James talks about meetings happening in the synagogue and doesn't use the word *church* (2:2).

How It's Built: James doesn't have the tight structure of Hebrews or the flowing, logical argument of Paul's letters. Instead, there are a series of related truths and practical teachings spread throughout the book.

Spicy Bible Controversy: This contrast with Paul's approach may be why some Christians over the centuries (including Martin Luther) have wondered whether James's practical teaching on good works might be in conflict with Paul's teachings on salvation by grace alone. In the end, it seems that James is emphasizing good works as evidence that someone is a Christian, and Paul is emphasizing that right standing with God is the gift of God alone and that good works can't help but flow from that. Paul and James knew each other, and James signed off on Paul's work in Acts 15, so we know they were on the same team, even when speaking into different situations in the early church.

"Twelve Tribes"?—Now That's a Name I Haven't Heard in a Long Time: James addresses his letter to "the twelve tribes scattered among the nations" (1:1). That's interesting, because we haven't heard God's chosen people called by that name for a long time.

The ten tribes of the Northern Kingdom had been gone since 722 BC (2 Kings 17), and the story of the Old Testament focuses on the remaining tribes of the Southern Kingdom of Judah after that. The oft-used biblical term *Jews* comes from *Judah*, so when the term *Jews* appears after the fall of the North, we're always talking about the tribes of Benjamin and Judah from the Southern Kingdom that were exiles in Babylon and Persia.

Because of that, it's noteworthy in Matthew 19 that Jesus talks about the twelve tribes of Israel together, as though they all still have some sort of future, even though ten of the tribes seem to be lost to history. It's also noteworthy that James specifically addresses his letter to the twelve tribes. The book of Revelation will pull on that thread later.

Student of Scripture: James has upward of twenty references to his brother's Sermon on the Mount (found in Matthew 5–7). In that sermon, Jesus introduces the idea of the kingdom of heaven and the values of that kingdom. It's got lots of memorable practical elements, and James leans into that. James also pulls in material from the law book of Leviticus and the practical wisdom book of Proverbs.

The Practical Stuff: James says your tongue can get you in trouble, and that Christians should keep that part of their life under control. He condemns the kind of class favoritism that happens all the time in the larger world but makes no sense in the church. He says that acting like you're the master of your own future and boasting about it is foolish. James tells Christians to communicate with kingdom values in mind—prioritizing listening and patience. There's more, but the gist is this: James clearly teaches that your faith in Jesus has to cause you to act like Jesus.

Faith Without Works Is Dead: Yep, he says it that explicitly in James 2:17: "Faith by itself, if it is not accompanied by action, is dead."

Tongues on Fire: In one of the passages that sounds most like it was lifted straight out of Proverbs, James draws on imagery reminiscent of the day of Pentecost in Acts 2 to talk about the power of the tongue and the importance of Christians demonstrating care with what they say: "Likewise, the tongue is a small part of the body, but it makes great boasts. Consider what a great forest is set on fire by a small spark. The tongue also is a fire, a world of evil among the parts of the body. It corrupts the whole body, sets the whole course of one's life on fire, and is itself set on fire by hell" (3:5–6).

Theme and Theme Verse: James 1:22—"Do not merely listen to the word, and so deceive yourselves. Do what it says."

When You Visualize James, Picture: The tongue.

VITAL STATS

Position: 60 of 66.
Chapters: 5.
Verses: 105.
Word Count: 1,684 (46/66).
Most-Used Words: God, Christ, suffering, glory, grace, hope.
Group: General Letters.
Audience: Gentile Christians in Asia Minor.
Written From: Rome (code name: Babylon).
Date: Early 60s AD.
Popularity Rank: 22 of 66.

Lightning-Fast Summary: Peter encourages persecuted Christians to stay strong, be shrewd about how they go about their business, and remain true to Jesus as a chosen holy people who are outsiders in the world.

Unique Feature: First Peter is the New Testament book that deals with the topic of persecution the most.

Who Wrote It? Confidently, Peter.

Original Language: Greek.

Writing Help? Scholars say the Greek in 1 Peter is noteworthy for its elegance. Though Peter's native language was Aramaic, he would have likely also spoken Greek. He may have been able to muster writing his letters on his own, or he may have had help from Silas or Mark, who were both excellent communicators and are both mentioned in the letter at the end of chapter 5.

Peter (Almost) Always Goes Big: Peter was the leader of Jesus' original disciples. He was loud, decisive, brash, and fiercely loyal to Jesus at every moment, except when Jesus needed him most. When Jesus was facing His final hours and praying in agony in Gethsemane, Peter fell asleep and failed to keep watch; then when Jesus was in the middle of His midnight trial, Peter denied knowing Him three times (Mark 14:32–42, 66–72). Still, Jesus propped Peter back up after the resurrection, and Peter went on to be one of the absolutely essential top-level figures in early Christianity.

When It Was Written: While intermittent local persecutions were breaking out against Christians around the Roman Empire, but before Emperor Nero began his harsh persecution of Christians in Rome itself. That puts it in the early 60s AD.

Secret Code Name for Rome: Peter says he's writing from "Babylon" (1 Peter 5:13), and he's not talking about the historic capital of ancient King Nebuchadnezzar's empire from six hundred years earlier. Literal Babylon was a loooong way in the wrong direction from all the action of the New Testament, and there's no reason to think Peter ever would have gone there. Instead, it is widely believed that "Babylon" is code for "Rome" in early Christian writing.

Original Audience: Peter specifically addresses Christians in five Roman provinces located in modern-day Turkey. Initially, Christians were met with indifference or curiosity, but as faith in Jesus gained popularity and Christians began to pull back from pagan worship and social customs, local persecutions became more common. Following Christ quickly turned costly for the believers whom Peter is writing to reassure.

You Know, I'm Something of a Persecuted Christian Myself: Peter was threatened by religious leaders, arrested several times, flogged, and eventually executed by Nero (who also executed Paul)—all for preaching about Jesus. So in 1 Peter, he writes as an expert on what persecution feels like, what it means, and what to do about it.

How It's Built: First Peter has practical teaching on how to live and contend with persecution, but all of that flows out of Peter's teaching about the true spiritual identity of Christians. He jumps back and forth between those two themes while weaving in the example of Jesus throughout the letter.

You're the People of God: Especially in chapters 1 and 2, Peter dips into Old Testament language to describe the persecuted church.

Peter calls God's people "exiles" and "foreigners," just like the Jews in Babylon and Persia. Peter says they're "chosen," just like God chose Abraham and his descendants. Peter says they're a "royal priesthood, a holy nation, God's special possession" (2:9)—just like God said about Israel in Exodus 19:5–6 when He pronounced, "Now if you obey me fully and keep my covenant, then out of all nations you will be my treasured possession. Although the whole earth is mine, you will be for me a kingdom of priests and a holy nation."

Peter tells them they weren't a people before, but now they're the "people of God" (2:10).

100 Percent Shrewd and 100 Percent Innocent: In this letter, Peter leans on a crucial teaching of Jesus that he himself had trouble internalizing at first. In Matthew 10:16, Jesus told Peter and the disciples, "I am sending you out like sheep among wolves. Therefore be as shrewd as snakes and as innocent as doves." These values aren't in competition with each other (as many modern readers like to imagine); instead, Jesus' instruction to His followers is that they be completely innocent but also completely shrewd, rather than find a false balance between the two values. Jesus *heavily* emphasized shrewdness—reading the room, understanding the moment, and being smart with resources.

Live Well: When Peter was flogged, he considered it a joyful blessing to suffer for Jesus, and he tells his readers the same is true for them (4:12–19). But he also tells them there's no blessing in suffering for acting like provocative idiots, so if you suffer, make sure it's for being Christlike. Throughout the letter, Peter tells them they have to keep order in their households, be good citizens, treat their neighbors with fairness and justice, and live godly and upright lives. If they do that, they're less likely to suffer and outsiders are more likely to become Christians. And ultimately, if they get persecuted anyway, then they're blessed for being counted worthy to suffer for the name of Jesus.

Most Famous Verses: 1 Peter 5:6–7—"Humble yourselves, therefore, under God's mighty hand, that he may lift you up in due time. Cast all your anxiety on him because he cares for you."

Theme of 1 Peter Spelled Out in One Passage: 1 Peter 2:9–12—"But you are a chosen people, a royal priesthood, a holy nation, God's special possession, that you may declare the praises of him who called you out of darkness into his wonderful light. Once you were not a people, but now you are the people of God; once you had not received mercy, but now you have received mercy. Dear friends, I urge you, as foreigners and exiles, to abstain from sinful desires, which wage war against your soul. Live such good lives among the pagans that, though they accuse you of doing wrong, they may see your good deeds and glorify God on the day he visits us."

When You Visualize 1 Peter, Picture: Babylon as Rome.

VITAL STATS

Position: 61 of 66.
Chapters: 3.
Verses: 61.
Word Count: 1,099 (55/66).
Most-Used Words: Lord, God, knowledge, righteousness, promise.
Group: General Letters.
Audience: Gentile Christians in Asia Minor.
Written From: Maybe Rome.
Date: Between AD 64 and 68.
Popularity Rank: 42 of 66.

Lightning-Fast Summary: Peter encourages Christians in Asia Minor to focus on God's grace, reject false teachers, and stay patient, but also to make themselves ready for Christ's return.

Unique Feature: Second Timothy is Paul's farewell letter, and 2 Peter serves the same purpose for Peter.

Who Wrote It? Peter, and he knows his days are numbered (1:13–14).

How Does He Know That? Two ways. First, Peter says Jesus made it clear to him that he'd soon put aside "the tent of this body" (1:13). Second, Peter could read the political situation and knew things were turning ugly in Rome. Rome burned in AD 64. At worst, Emperor Nero orchestrated it to grab land; at best, Nero botched the response to the crisis. Either way, he found a convenient scapegoat in the misunderstood Christians. He was turning up the heat on the church, and Peter was the most prominent Christian in Rome. Peter was on a collision course with execution.

When It Was Written: Nero committed suicide on June 9, AD 68, but not before having Peter executed sometime between AD 64–67. That puts the date for this letter between the beginning of Nero's persecutions in AD 64 and his death in AD 68.

Stuff You Can Still Physically Look At: There's a church in Rome right next to the Colosseum and Nero's gardens called San Pietro in Vincoli (Saint Peter in Chains). At the front, they've got a set of ancient Roman shackles purported to have been worn by Peter.

Original Audience: Probably the same group of Christians as 1 Peter, most of whom were probably Gentiles.

Why the Letter? Peter has been hearing reports of false teachers in Asia Minor who were living morally sloppy lives and justifying it with made-up theology. Also, Peter is nearing the end of his life, and he wants to give God's people words to keep with them after he dies. He comes right out and says that in 1:15: "And I will make every effort to see that after my departure you will always be able to remember these things."

Like a Bunch of Paul's Letters in One: Peter stresses the grace of Jesus (like Paul did in Galatians and Ephesians), the importance of rejecting false teachers (like Paul did in 1 Timothy and Titus), and the fact of Christ's coming return (like Paul did in 1 and 2 Thessalonians).

It's Also like Jude: Chapter 2 of 2 Peter has a ton in common with the book of Jude. It's not clear whether Peter was referencing Jude, or the other way around.

Peter Says Paul's Letters Are Scripture: That Peter and Paul say a lot of the same stuff isn't an accident. The two knew each other and had at least one tense moment together (referenced in Galatians 2). Peter is aware of Paul's letters and refers to them as Scripture in chapter 3: "Bear in mind that our Lord's patience means salvation, just as our dear brother Paul also wrote you with the wisdom that God gave him. He writes the same way in all his letters, speaking in them of these matters. His letters contain some things that are hard to understand, which ignorant and unstable people distort, as they do the other Scriptures, to their own destruction" (vv. 15–16).

Feed My Sheep: Peter publicly disowned Jesus three times during Jesus' most difficult hour (Matthew 26:69–75), but Jesus restored him and matched the number of Peter's denials, telling him three times to feed His sheep (John 21:15–17). No doubt, Peter was making every effort to care for Jesus' flock with what little time he had left, and to do it in a way that would last beyond his death.

Most Famous Verse: 2 Peter 3:9—"The Lord is not slow in keeping his promise, as some understand slowness. Instead he is patient with you, not wanting anyone to perish, but everyone to come to repentance."

Theme Verse: 2 Peter 1:3—"His divine power has given us everything we need for a godly life through our knowledge of him who called us by his own glory and goodness."

When You Visualize 2 Peter, Picture: Peter in chains.

The chains of Saint Peter, in the Church of San Pietro in Vincoli in Rome, Italy.
e55evu/stock.adobe.com

1 JOHN

VITAL STATS

Position: 62 of 66.
Chapters: 5.
Verses: 105.
Word Count: 2,141 (41/66).
Most-Used Words: Love, know, God, sin, light.
Group: General Letters.
Audience: Christians everywhere.
Written From: Probably Ephesus.
Date: 80s or 90s AD.
Popularity Rank: 25 of 66.

Lightning-Fast Summary: John, the disciple, writes to an undisclosed church, graciously and joyfully reminding them Jesus is fully God and fully human and equipping them with a threefold test to know what's true.

Unique Feature: First John closely matches the gospel of John's style and tone. The audience was probably already very familiar with John's gospel, and the opening lines of both books are clearly meant to complement each other.

Type of Book: Even though 1 John is lumped in with the General Letters section of the New Testament, it's really more of a personal sermon sent the way one would send a letter. In many ways, 1 John is simply a sermon distilled from the gospel of John.

Who Wrote It? John the son of Zebedee, who also wrote the gospel of John, 2 John, 3 John, and Revelation.

When It Was Written: John is the only disciple who lived to old age and wasn't martyred. He wrote this letter when he was well into his grandfatherly stage of life, before he died around AD 100.

Original Audience: John doesn't greet anyone by name, and he doesn't say exactly what church he's sending it to. Wherever this church was, it's clear it was a well-established community of Christians who were having trouble with a heretical teaching called Gnosticism.

The Specter of Gnosticism: Gnosticism was the most popular heresy in the early church, and the biggest threat to true Christianity. It had roots in the first century but really blew up in the second century. It was a mashup of Greek and Christian ideas that took on several forms, including Docetism. The Gnostics thought that everything is built out of opposites in tension—like on and off, light and dark, love and hate. They believed that the physical is evil, and the spiritual is good; therefore the body is bad, and the soul or spirit is good. Some Gnostics played out their disdain for the physical by denying their bodies any comfort or pleasure, while others indulged anything that made their bodies feel good. They had a problem with the idea of God taking on flesh.

Phantom Jesus: Some of these false teachers were saying that Jesus never really had a body and that He didn't really die, but only seemed to die a physical death. This heresy is called Docetism. The Docetists might have believed Jesus was divine in some way, but they didn't believe He was fully God and fully human, and therefore He didn't really die for the forgiveness of sins.

The Spirit of 1 John: Yes, there's a problem, but John isn't panicking. His letter is calm and proactive, providing fatherly encouragement and equipping the church with tools for recognizing the good things that are from God. It's warm and joyful.

Fellowship, Joy, Obedience, and Forgiveness: In the first section, John says those four great things are why he's writing the letter. John reminds the church that he saw, heard, and even touched the story of Jesus firsthand. It's real, and they should be unified and hopeful because of that.

John wants them to remember that God isn't half dark and half light, like some Gnostics' misguided conception of balance required. Rather, "God is light; in him there is no darkness at all" (1:5). When we walk with God, we walk in the light—purified by the blood of Jesus.

Threefold Test: John gives the church a threefold test to know if someone or something is from God. True Christians will (1) acknowledge

Jesus as the Christ, (2) obey God's commands, and (3) love other Christians. True teachings will promote the same. It's a simple, memorable test the church will be able to use long after John is gone, and John spends the rest of the book cycling through these three tests.

One More Reason to Write: John wrapped up the gospel of John by saying he wrote it so that "you may believe that Jesus is the Messiah, the Son of God, and that by believing you may have life in his name" (John 20:31). Very similarly, John concludes 1 John by saying, "I write these things to you who believe in the name of the Son of God so that you may know that you have eternal life" (5:13).

Why Christians Have Creeds: It's easy to see how Gnostic ideas could sow confusion and moral chaos in a church. Eventually, the pressure of Gnosticism forced early Christians to refine their theology into airtight statements of true Christian beliefs called creeds.

The Gospel in 1 John: It's everywhere, but the whole thing comes through tightly in 1 John 1:5–7—"This is the message we have heard from him and declare to you: God is light; in him there is no darkness at all. If we claim to have fellowship with him and yet walk in the darkness, we lie and do not live out the truth. But if we walk in the light, as he is in the light, we have fellowship with one another, and the blood of Jesus, his Son, purifies us from all sin."

When You Visualize 1 John, Picture: Light.

VITAL STATS

Position: 63 of 66.
Chapters: 1.
Verses: 13.
Word Count: 245 (65/66).
Most-Used Words: Truth, love, commandment, walk, teaching.
Group: General Letters.
Audience: The chosen lady and her children.
Written From: Probably Ephesus.
Date: 80s or 90s AD.

2 JOHN

Popularity Rank: 64 of 66.

Lightning-Fast Summary: A letter from John telling Christians not to welcome false teachers.

Unique Feature: The letter is addressed to "the lady chosen by God and to her children" (v. 1). It's probably the strangest salutation of any of the New Testament letters.

Who Is That? The context dictates that "the lady chosen by God" is a local church. John doesn't say which one, but he lived in and wielded great influence around Ephesus at the end of his life, so it was probably a church near there, or maybe even the Ephesian church herself.

Who Wrote It? It's John again. Even in just thirteen verses, there're plenty of signature similarities to 1 John.

Who Sent It? The letter was written by John, but verse 13 indicates it was sent by a sister church.

An Anti-Letter of Recommendation: Paul, the apostles, and the churches used letters of recommendation to vouch for true teachers, reliable gospel partners, and good churches. Paul alludes to this in 2 Corinthians 3, and Apollos gets a letter of recommendation from the Ephesian church in Acts 18:27. In 2 John, we see the opposite of this practice—a letter saying *not to receive* false teachers who are on their way.

Deceivers: John warns about false teachers who peddle the heretical idea that Jesus was a phantom who never took on flesh and never actually died (this is called Docetism). John doesn't mince words: "Any such person is the deceiver and the antichrist" (v. 7).

Hospitality for Traveling Teachers: In Matthew 10, Jesus sent out His earliest disciples with miraculous power and a message even simpler than Jonah's: "The kingdom of heaven has come near" (v. 7). He told them to seek out peaceful, receptive people and stay with them while they told them and their neighbors the message of the kingdom. Paul and the apostles stayed with Christians along the way, and many New Testament letters instruct their recipients to receive a minister of the gospel.

No Hospitality for Traveling False Teachers: Second John makes it clear these deceivers shouldn't be allowed to teach, and they also should be denied hospitality. John writes, "Whoever continues in the teaching [of Christ] has both the Father and the Son. If anyone comes to you and does not bring this teaching, do not take them into your house or welcome them. Anyone who welcomes them shares in their wicked work" (vv. 9–11).

That's That: Seventy-five percent of this short letter is joyful and celebratory of the grace and love of Jesus and the Father. In the middle, there're a few verses that get down to the unpleasant business described above, but John doesn't linger. He wraps up the matter and concludes warmly, and that's that.

This Is Love: A highly applicable follow-up verse to 1 John is 2 John verse 6—"And this is love: that we walk in obedience to his commands. As you have heard from the beginning, his command is that you walk in love."

When You Visualize 2 John, Picture: A "No Vacancy" sign.

VITAL STATS

Position: 64 of 66.
Chapters: 1.
Verses: 14.
Word Count: 219 (66/66).
Most-Used Words: Truth, love, good, evil, hospitality, testimony.
Group: General Letters.
Audience: A church leader named Gaius.
Written From: Probably Ephesus.
Date: 80s or 90s AD.
Popularity Rank: 61 of 66.

Lightning-Fast Summary: John writes to a church leader named Gaius to say thanks for receiving the reliable teachers John had sent. John also calls out a guy named Diotrephes, who rejects the teachers John sent.

Unique Feature: This is the shortest book of the Bible by word count. It's a simple letter that says what it needs to say, and nothing more.

Who Wrote It? John the son of Zebedee, one of the twelve original disciples and the author of the gospel of John, Revelation, and 1, 2, and 3 John.

There's huge consistency in writing style, themes, and verbiage among all five of these books.

Original Audience: It's addressed to a good guy named Gaius whom John calls faithful. John thanks Gaius for trusting John's letters of recommendation and receiving the traveling teachers John has vouched for.

A Guy So Bad It Prompted a Whole Book of the Bible: Diotrephes was another leader in Gaius's church (probably in the orbit of Ephesus). Diotrephes has some sort of problem with John, and he mistreats the traveling teachers John vouches for and doesn't even seem to want John to come visit.

He's a selfish gossip, and John's going to deal with him when he comes to town.

A Man Who Loved to Be First: Several characters in the Bible have beautiful descriptive labels forever linked to their names (the fancy term is *epithets*). Abraham *believed God and it was credited to him as righteousness.* David was *a man after God's own heart.* John was *the disciple whom Jesus loved.* These are amazing things to be remembered for! Well, old Diotrephes gets his own timeless reputational label in 3 John verse 9, and it's not great: "I wrote to the church, but Diotrephes, *who loves to be first,* will not welcome us" (emphasis added).

The Point: Third John reiterates the recommendation system that had ensured proper teaching for decades, and it places a premium on doing what is good and true. Also, it's probably best for Christians to be hospitable to one another in general as a marker of being forgiven by Christ and a part of His family of faith.

Most Applicable Verse for Modern Audiences: 3 John verse 11—"Dear friend, do not imitate what is evil but what is good. Anyone who does what is good is from God. Anyone who does what is evil has not seen God."

Theme Verse: 3 John verse 8—"We ought therefore to show hospitality to such people so that we may work together for the truth."

When You Visualize 3 John, Picture: Diotrephes, a man who loved to be first.

VITAL STATS

Position: 65 of 66.
Chapters: 1.
Verses: 25.
Word Count: 461 (62/66).
Most-Used Words: Ungodly, faith, Lord, Jesus, mercy, judgment.
Group: General Letters.
Audience: Christians.
Written From: Unknown.
Date: Before AD 68 (and maybe way earlier than that).
Popularity Rank: 59 of 66.

Lightning-Fast Summary: A letter by Jude to help Christians see through the false teachers who were infiltrating churches and fooling believers.

Unique Feature: This little letter alludes to one legendary extrabiblical work and directly quotes another. More on that in a minute.

Who Wrote It? Jude, who identifies himself as a brother of James. If that is James the brother of Jesus and leader of the Jerusalem church, then Jude would also be a half brother of Jesus who grew up in the household of Mary and Joseph.

Jude Is a Lot like 2 Peter: Second Peter 2 has a lot in common with Jude. One clearly influences the other, which demonstrates how the New Testament came together organically in the very early days of the church. Christians believe that God guided the whole process to make the Bible exactly what He wanted it to be.

Original Audience: Christians in general. Jude doesn't greet a specific church or any individuals. It's a general letter meant to be copied and circulated among churches and Christians.

Change of Plans: Jude opens by saying that although he was eager to "write to you about the salvation we share, I felt compelled to write and urge you to contend for the faith that was once for all entrusted to God's holy people" (v. 3). Jude goes on to sound the alarm over infiltrators who "have secretly slipped in among you" (v. 4). Apparently, these wolves in sheep's clothing twisted the Christian understanding of Jesus' grace to justify horrible, indulgent behavior and invited their brothers and sisters to join them.

Jude's Heated: After laying out the crisis, Jude draws on biblical and extrabiblical examples of God harshly judging people who twist and manipulate the holy things of God. Jude calls these people "grumblers and faultfinders" who "follow their own evil desires" and brag about themselves and then flatter and manipulate others (v. 16).

Closing with Coaching: Jude wraps up by saying it's no surprise that people like this will show up, but don't imitate them or be divided by them. In all of it, he urges, "By building yourselves up in your most holy faith and praying in the Holy Spirit, keep yourselves in God's love as you wait for the mercy of our Lord Jesus Christ to bring you to eternal life" (vv. 20–21).

The Book of Enoch: Jude quotes from the noncanonical book of 1 Enoch in verses 14 and 15. His audience probably knew this book well, and Jude takes the opportunity to deftly suggest that 1 Enoch points to Jesus, even if it isn't Scripture.

Lots of quotes and references to extrabiblical books happen throughout the Bible. Paul quotes three secular philosophers in his letters (Aratus, Menander, and Epimenides), and the Old Testament references a bunch of chronicles of different kings and kingdoms, as well as something called the Book of Jasher.

Jude's Famous Doxology: Jude concludes with a closing blessing (called a benediction) that has been repeated by Christians for two thousand years. It goes like this: "To him who is able to keep you from stumbling and to present you before his glorious presence without fault and with great joy—to the only God our Savior be glory, majesty, power and authority, through Jesus Christ our Lord, before all ages, now and forevermore! Amen" (vv. 24–25).

When You Visualize Jude, Picture: A wolf in sheep's clothing.

VITAL STATS

Position: 66 of 66.
Chapters: 22.
Verses: 404.
Word Count: 9,851 (25/66).
Most-Used Words: Lamb, throne, angel, beast, seven, God, heaven, earth, book, seal, dragon, kingdom, judgment.
Group: Apocalypse.
Audience: Seven specific churches and also everyone.
Written From: Island of Patmos.
Date: mid-90s AD.
Popularity Rank: 12 of 66.

REVELATION

Lightning-Fast Summary: Revelation is the summary of the theology of the Bible and the final chapter of the Old and New Testaments that tells the end of the story of history and God's redemptive plan in the world.

Unique Feature: The previous twenty-one New Testament books are all letters from great leaders of the early church. In the first section of Revelation, there are seven more letters, but these are from Jesus Himself. We've seen hints of churches and individuals ignoring letters from John and other apostles (Diotrephes in 3 John, for example), but in Revelation, it's Jesus who is writing, and that can't be ignored. Jesus weighing in after the twenty-one New Testament epistles is reminiscent of when God shows up to settle the discussion at the end of Job.

Time: In Genesis, the Bible story starts before time as we know it began, and in Revelation, we follow the story to the end of this age of existence. God transcends all of that. In Revelation, He says about Himself, "I am the Alpha and the Omega, the Beginning and the End" (21:6).

Symmetry: Genesis shows that at the beginning of the story, God and humanity were together in a perfect creation untouched by sin and death. Revelation shows that at the end of the story, God and a restored humanity will be back together in a perfect creation that has been purged of sin and death. The story is tragic and difficult in the middle, but Revelation gives us a beautiful ending earned at God's expense.

Controversy: People debate, speculate, and argue about Revelation more than any other book of the Bible. Revelation offers a tantalizing and terrifying glimpse into the future. If you've read the Bible, it's impossible *not* to think about how the story will wrap up.

Terrifying but Joyful: Because of that understandable eagerness and the complexity and intensity of the debates surrounding how best to read Revelation, it can be easy to forget the fact that Revelation is a book about God's joyful final victory over sin, evil, and death. In Revelation, God's wrath against evil is terrifying, but even more stunning is the beautiful, perfect redemption He accomplishes and invites His people into.

Helpful Opening Line: Revelation 1:1–3 tells us (1) what the book is, (2) who wrote it, (3) what it's about, (4) how it was made, (5) who it's for, and (6) what happens to people who read it. It's hard to ask for more clarity than that.

The first three verses go like this: "The revelation from Jesus Christ, which God gave him to show his servants what must soon take place. He made it known by sending his angel to his servant John, who testifies to everything he saw—that is, the word of God and the testimony of Jesus Christ. Blessed is the one who reads aloud the words of this prophecy, and blessed are those who hear it and take to heart what is written in it, because the time is near."

What Is Revelation? It's a unique genre of writing called an apocalypse. In the original Greek, the second word of the book is *apokalypsis* (translated as "revelation" in English). In movies and television shows, the word *apocalypse* is usually associated with world-ending calamities, but in this book, it literally means "revealing" or "unveiling." Revelation is briefly going to pull back the curtain on the heavenly realm and on future things.

Who Wrote It? It's the revelation of Jesus Himself, and it's recorded and relayed by John the son of Zebedee, the disciple whom Jesus loved who also wrote the gospel of John and 1, 2, and 3 John.

What It's About: What must "soon take place" (1:1). The completion of history and God's redemptive plan was in motion when Revelation was written, is still in motion as you're reading this, and will fully finish playing out later.

How It Was Made: Jesus sent His angel to John, who is testifying to everything he saw.

Who It's For: Revelation is for anyone who reads it.

What Happens to the Reader? Anyone who reads Revelation, hears it, and takes it to heart is blessed.

Seven Churches: The first three chapters read like a hybrid of Paul's letters and prophetic stuff from Isaiah or Ezekiel. John, writing from the island of Patmos, offers a greeting in the style of the New Testament letters and then describes Jesus showing up and telling John to write what he sees and send it to seven specific churches in Asia Minor. The letters to the seven churches are each only a few verses long and are a mix of blessings and warnings.

Now the End-of-Time Stuff Starts: After the letters are written, Jesus says to John, "Come up here, and I will show you what must take place after this" (4:1). From here until the end of the book, we're looking ahead. Sometimes the imagery is hard to visualize, but the gist is always understandable.

The Lamb and the Scroll: There's a key character who keeps showing up throughout the whole story: It's a Lamb who has been slain but is alive again. In chapter 5, there's an important scroll that's sealed with seven seals, and only the Lamb is worthy to break the seals and open the scroll. A heavenly elder by the throne of God calls the Lamb "the Lion of the tribe of Judah" and "the Root of David" (that's Jesus). Then in chapter 6, the Lamb breaks open six of the seals on that scroll, and each time He does, new judgments happen in the world. Then twelve thousand from all twelve tribes of Israel show up, along with tons of people from all the nations, and they praise God together, just like all those Old Testament prophets predict. After that, everything is totally quiet as the Lamb cracks open the last seal on the scroll (chapter 7). This uncorks a series of judgments on the world, including an army of locust-men, like the Old Testament prophet Joel predicted when he talked about the day of the Lord. The judgments keep coming—wave after wave—and many die, but the nations don't repent (chapters 8–10).

Two Great Witnesses and Two Great Evils: Two great witnesses show up in Jerusalem to point everyone to God, but the city rejects them, just like they rejected Jesus. They're killed, and their bodies are left in the street, but God raises them to life (chapter 11). After that rejection, God sends more judgments on the nations and presses ahead to defeat two great evils that have wreaked havoc since the beginning of Genesis—the ancient serpent, who is Satan himself, and the nations, which are the unjust worldly powers that have set themselves up as gods. The day of the Lord is terrifying, but in it God defeats both Satan (portrayed as a dragon) and the nations (portrayed as Babylon).

The Throne of Judgment and the Book of Life: In Revelation 20, God sits on His great white throne and issues His final judgments. We know from all of Scripture (and from experience) that everyone is guilty, but those who are clothed in Christ's righteousness, as Paul talks about in Romans, will be declared innocent. At the white throne judgment, everyone who is in Christ—whose name is in the Book of Life—is welcomed into a new heaven and a new earth, where God dwells with His people forever, untouched by sin, pain, and death.

The Redemptive Plan Is Complete; the Curse Is Defeated: After that, the heaven and earth we live in pass away, and God makes new ones, undamaged by sin (chapter 21). After all that, God and humanity are back together. The declaration of victory goes like this: "Look! God's dwelling place is now among the people, and he will dwell with them. They will be his people, and God himself will be with them and be their God. 'He will wipe every tear from their eyes. There will be no more death or mourning or crying or pain, for the old order of things has passed away" (21:3–4).

The Cave of the Apocalypse on the island of Patmos.

giumas/stock.adobe.com

There is a new Jerusalem and something that looks like a new Eden. God is there, and the water of life flows from His throne (just like the prophecy in Ezekiel 47), and there's no temple because "the Lord God Almighty and the Lamb are its temple" (Revelation 21:22).

Satan is crushed. The human problem is solved. The curse is defeated. God and humanity made in His image are together in full forever.

It Is Done: After all that, God says, "It is done" (21:6). It's reminiscent of Jesus' words on the cross: "It is finished" (John 19:30).

Author's Note: Revelation has a little epilogue at the very end where Jesus and the messenger angel remind John that all of this is true, and that the person who keeps these words will receive the gift of the water of life. There's a closing warning against adding to or subtracting from this message, so as someone who just finished summarizing this book, I think it's important to remind you that this chapter is no substitute for the real thing, and you should definitely *go read it all for yourself.*

But If You Really Don't Have Time to Read the Whole Thing, at Least Read: Revelation 5 and Revelation 18–22.

Key Verses: Revelation 1:7–8—"'Look, he is coming with the clouds,' and 'every eye will see him, even those who pierced him'; and all peoples on earth 'will mourn because of him.' So shall it be! Amen. 'I am the Alpha and the Omega,' says the Lord God, 'who is, and who was, and who is to come, the Almighty.'"

When You Visualize Revelation, Picture: Jesus standing on the freshly crushed serpent and there's a new heaven and a new earth.

ACKNOWLEDGMENTS

I put the fingers to the keys, but this book exists because of a bunch of other people.

I'm grateful to my parents, Rex and Sue Whitman, and to my brother, Mark, and sister, Kendra, for making a household where we thought about and talked about the Bible in normal conversation like normal humans all the time. I'm grateful to my father-in-law and mother-in-law, Dennis and Caroline Ritchey, for coming at it the same way.

I'm thankful to Destin Sandlin for helping me figure out how to take the tone of those normal household Bible conversations to a larger living room. I also owe my friends Aron Utecht and Mike Harding a debt of gratitude for reviewing the manuscript in its clumsy formative stages. My friend Jeff Foote edits my podcast. We talk Bible together endlessly, and those things mean the world to me. I'll always be indebted to Bethany Gano, who has lent sincerity of heart and an artful eye to my work from the beginning. Thanks to Meg Brummer for helping me pull together years of my notes. I also owe a debt to Dr. John Monson and other scholar friends who were kind enough to answer all of my most peculiar questions. I feel huge gratitude to so many other friends as well.

I appreciate my agent, Dan Balow, for pushing me to make this happen and for being so patient while I tried out all my jokes on him. I'm also grateful to Dan for connecting me with my publisher, Zondervan. They have provided a wonderful experience. I'm thankful to my editor, Andrea Palpant, for being a smart, fun, creative partner who did nothing but make this book better every time she touched it. Also, shout-outs to Dirk Buursma for doing the careful line-editing and rooting for this book with sincerity, as well as to Kait Lamphere for making this book look cool.

I owe a particular debt of gratitude to all the people who watch my YouTube videos and who listen to *The Ten Minute Bible Hour Podcast*. I read the Bible more and understand it better because a bunch of people are willing to spend time studying it with me every day. I'm hugely thankful for the way this group of people has shaped my life.

My three kids are my favorite three kids of all the kids ever, and no matter how hard I try to explain it, they'll never fully know how much they mean to me.

Most of all, I wrote this book because I believe that the actual God who made everything and who still cares about the world is behind the Bible, and I wanted to take a swing at showing you how beautifully it all hangs together and points back to Him. Faith was easy for me at first, then cripplingly hard, and now fresh and real in ways I couldn't have pictured before. No one has helped me in that journey more than my gentle Camilla, who taught me grace in the face of crushing doubt and who shows me daily what a life infused with the values of Christ looks like. She, more than anyone, deserves credit for this book.

From the Publisher

GREAT BOOKS

ARE EVEN BETTER WHEN THEY'RE SHARED!

Help other readers find this one

- Post a review at your favorite online bookseller
- Post a picture on a social media account and share why you enjoyed it
- Send a note to a friend who would also love it—or better yet, give them a copy

Thanks for reading!

www.ingramcontent.com/pod-product-compliance
Lightning Source LLC
LaVergne TN
LVHW020152100826
845372LV00020B/441

* 9 7 8 0 3 1 0 3 6 9 7 6 9 *